Eyewitness Accounts of the American Revolution

The Journal of Claude Blanchard

Translated by William Duane

Edited by Thomas Balch

The New York Times & Arno Press

THE JOURNAL

OF

CLAUDE BLANCHARD,

COMMISSARY OF THE FRENCH AUXILIARY ARMY SENT
TO THE UNITED STATES DURING THE
AMERICAN REVOLUTION.

1780--1783.

𝕿ranslated from a 𝔉rench 𝔐anuscript,

BY WILLIAM DUANE,

AND

EDITED BY THOMAS BALCH.

ALBANY, J. MUNSELL.

1876.

CONTENTS.

CHAPTER I.

CHAPTER II.

CHAPTER III.

CHAPTER IV.

[In the original, the Table of Contents is continued no farther.]

EDITOR'S PREFACE.

During a sojourn of some years in Europe I occupied myself in collecting books, engravings or other materials for a contribution to American and French history, the subject of which did not seem to me to have been thoroughly studied or fairly narrated. It was intended that the work should be a careful history of the part taken by the French in the American war for independence. The first part of the work, giving a history of the expeditionary corps under Rochambeau, from its embarkation to its return, with a full narrative of the military operations in which it was engaged, was published in Paris in 1872 [1] The second part, containing notices of the regiments and fleets, and of the officers who served in our cause, whether as volunteers, or under the orders of the French government, is now ready and will shortly appear in that city.

Most of the sources from which I derived the materials for these volumes were manuscripts, several of which are

---

[1] Paris, A. Sauton; Philadelphia, J. B. Lippincott.

enumerated in an opening chapter of the part already published. [1] One of these is presented in the following pages,
to the students of American history. As we learn from
Mr. Blanchard's own preface, it is truly a Journal in
which were noted down almost daily such military, social
or political incidents as seemed to him of sufficient importance to be recorded for the instruction of his children, or
for his own reminiscences in later life.

This manuscript came into my hands through the kindness of its possessor, Mr. Maurice La Chesnais, the great
grandson of its author. To him I am also indebted for the
information which enables me to give a notice of Mr.
Blanchard.

Claude Blanchard, a descendant of one of the noble
French families, was born at Angers the 16 May, 1742.
In 1762 he entered the ministry of war " under the orders
of one of his relatives," Mr. Dubois, the chief of the
bureaux in the War Department, who also held other
responsible positions. In 1768 Blanchard was named war-
commissary, and remained in Corsica for ten years with
this rank. He was promoted for his services, and in 1780
was sent as commissary-in-chief with General Rochambeau

---

[1] *Les Français en Amérique*, pp. 6 – 17.

to America. In his Journal we have incidentally an account
of the duties of his office. In 1788 he was sent to Arras,
where he was called upon to act as commander of the
National Guard, and was soon sent to the legislative
assembly as its representative together with Carnot, then
wholly obscure though since so well known for the part
which he subsequently played in the unhappy drama of
the French revolution. In the assembly Mr. Blanchard
exercised his functions unobtrusively but discreetly and so
far gained the favorable consideration of his fellow-legis-
lators, that he was the most frequent chairman of military
committees, making the reports on these questions, an
honor which was shared between him, General Lacueé and
Mathieu Dumas. He was deprived of his position as
commissary by the committee of public safety, but later,
after their fall, he became chief commissary to the army
of the Sambre and Meuse, then to the army of the Interior,
and lastly to the Hotel des Invalides, where he died in
1802, leaving to his family " an honorable name, and the
reputation of remarkable virtues and talents." Such
at least was the language in which General Beranger announced his death. The first consul, on hearing of his
decease, expressed his regrets in warm and feeling terms.[1]

---

[1] *Revue Militaire Française.* 1869. p. 373.

Many matters of interest will be found in the following pages concerning the organization and discipline of both branches of the French service. The bad food, the filthy, black water, the ravages of the scurvy, the frequent deaths, testify to the character of the one ; the insubordination of the officers, the duels, often fatal : " a man-slayer," says Blanchard, " but it was my fate to meet them everywhere ;" do not present an attractive picture of the other. It may be inferred that Custine's violence was the sole act of the kind which occurred, and let us hope that insolent as de Marigny's answer was, yet that it was not by his hand de Ternay lost his life, but that the unhappy commander died of fever, as Mr. Blanchard was informed he did.[1]

Interesting as Mr. Blanchard's Journal is, it gives but few military details. The Journal of Count de Menonville is, on the other hand, full and minute in this respect. So is the Narrative of the Baron du Bourg, who also recounts the incidents which passed in the " military family " of de Rochambeau. Du Petit Thouars tells the story of the campaigns of d'Estaing and de Grasse. Prince de Broglie's Relation (of which I have the translation ready for the

---

[1] In some of the other manuscripts the brighter side of the French character is agreeably depicted.

press), gives sprightly and entertaining pictures of society in Philadelphia, Newport and Boston. [1] The Comte de Pontgibaud describes his adventures whilst aid-de-camp to La Fayette, and those with which he met later when he and others came to America to escape the guillotine. This collection of manuscripts, together with extracts of documents which I found in the archives of the French war and navy departments, form a full and circumstantial history of the French military and naval operations in America whilst they were acting as our allies.

I have added a few notes to the Journal, and at first purposed giving a historical sketch of the various regiments and biographical notices of the officers taken from the manuscript of a volume, as yet unpublished, which I have prepared partly from the French archives, partly from other and diversified sources of information. But it was feared that such a mass of notes would make the book rather heavy, and they were laid aside. Much and interesting information concerning the regiments can be found in the excellent works of Gen. Suzanne [2]

---

[1] I would be much pleased to obtain a copy of the *Verses in French* addressed by Mrs. Tudor to Marie Antoinette, of which the Prince de Broglie makes mention, but which my researches have thus far failed to discover

[2] *Histoire de l' Ancienne Infanterie Française*, par le General Suzanne, Paris, 1853, 8 vols. with atlas. *La Cavalerie Française*, 2 vols., Paris, 1874

B

The choice of de Rochambeau as the commander of the
auxiliary army-corps was due to the wise and unselfish
counsels of La Fayette, and it was fortunate for the cause
of the Americans that so skillful a stategist was selected.
The well known compliment addressed to him by Napoleon
was fully deserved, and the part which he took in the campaign which terminated our war is a proof of its justice.
The appointment of de Ternay was probably due to
similar influences. But the fidelity with which that con-
scientious officer executed his orders led to unhappy results
for him. He sacrificed everything to the successful convoy
and landing of the troops. Twice during the voyage he
refused to deliver battle with English squadrons when, as
subsequent events showed, he would certainly have been
victorious. The reproaches of his captains were bitter.
The stings of his own wounded pride were unbearable.
They produced and aggravated a fever which ended his
life. But the king recognized his meritorious self-abne-
gation, and ordered a monument to be erected to his memory, bearing an inscription fairly and honorably earned
by him who slept beneath the stone.[1] Republican grati-

[1] The original inscription in Latin and a translation into English, the
particulars of de Ternay's death, the funeral ceremonies, and the facts connected with the restoration of the monument, are narrated in an eloquent

tude allowed it to fall into decay; but fortunately, in
1873, the Marquis de .Noailles, then French envoy at
Washington, visited Newport, and with the permission of
his government, and at its expense, had the monument re-
constructed. On the motion of Senator Anthony a bill
was passed to repay these expenses, but the French government declined the offer. The sum voted was there-
upon converted by congress into a fund for the future
preservation of the monument, and thus, though tardily,
has been secured the tribute due to the memory of one of
the many gallant Frenchmen who sacrificed their lives to
secure the independence of America.

Some glimpses also of American society appear in the
Journal: the impression produced by General Washington's appearance and manners, General Varnum's conversation in Latin, the hospitality of Lady Washington
and of Mrs. Greene, the beauty of Mrs. Temple and other
ladies, Madeira and toasts, the schools, the churches, the
psalm-singing, the ragged and unshod soldiers, the taste
for porcelain, the men spending whole days by their fire-

---

speech by Senator Anthony on introducing a bill, Dec. 16, 1873, to pay the
expenses of reconstructing the monument to the Chevalier de Ternay. *Me-
morial Addresses* delivered in the United States senate by Henry B. Anthony. Providence, 1875.

xii

sides and wives ; these, and many similar incidents, give us quite an insight into the American life of that day, as it presented itself to the eyes of a French gentleman, rather ceremonious in his manners and rigid in his principles. He more than once mentions the beauty of the females, more often their innocence and simplicity. Their descendants have reason to be proud of them. In all the manuscripts which I have in hand, written by these European soldiers of divers temperaments and characters, a profound, almost reverential, testimony is borne to the graceful manners, the native dignity, the unsullied conduct, the moral purity of the American women.

Mr. Blanchard prepared a preface to his manuscript, of which a translation, due likewise to the pen of Mr. Duane, who has so admirably " rendered into English" the Journal itself, is herewith given.

PREFACE.

I was employed for three years, as chief commissary, with the troops which M. de Rochambeau led to the assistance of the Americans. During all that war, I wrote down, almost every day, the events which I witnessed, and those which concerned myself. This journal is not in very good order, and now that I have some leisure (Messidor of the year II of the French republic), I am about to make a fair copy of it, without changing anything in the style and form. If I should make any new reflections, I will say so, though this information is quite useless, for positively I am writing only for myself and with the view of turning my leisure to some account.

Before commencing this journal, I ought to give an idea of the United States of America; besides, I find this notice in my journal, and I wrote it at the time of the departure of the expedition.

The country comprised in the United States of America extends along the eastern coast of North America, from latitude 46° to 30°, that is, for about three hundred and ten leagues; but it has not an equal breadth, for in many

places it does not extend more than sixty leagues; and
the population of this country is not in proportion to its
size. The inhabitants are reckoned to be about three
millions. The provinces, beginning with those to the
north, are New Hampshire, Massachusetts, wherein is
Boston, Connecticut, Rhode Island, New York, Pennsylvania, wherein is Philadelphia, the seat of the congress,
Maryland, Delaware, Virginia, North Carolina, South
Carolina, and Georgia, wherein is Savannah.[1]

There are several islands forming parts of some of these
provinces, such as Long Island. The troops of the English
royalists are chiefly stationed in New York; they also
have many places in Carolina, some troops in Georgia and
especially at Savannah. [This was written in the early
part of 1780.]

To the northward and westward of the thirteen provinces
is Canada, which belonged to France, and which she ceded
to England by the last treaty of peace, that of 1762. South
of the thirteen provinces is Florida, also ceded to England
by Spain, which France indemnified by giving to her her
possessions upon the Mississippi and the Gulf of Mexico.

Besides these possessions of the English, which form a
bow around the thirteen states, of which Clinton's army
in New Jersey resembles the end of the arrow, there are
also some savage nations which sometimes attack and

---

[1] The writer omits New Jersey.

plunder the subjects of the United States. Let us now consider these states. Each of the thirteen provinces has its
own council, its own militia, and its own laws; each sends
a deputy to the general assembly, otherwise known as the
congress, which is held at Philadelphia. Over this congress,
a deputy from one of the provinces presides in turn.

It is the congress that directs the operations of the nation
which makes alliances, receives the envoys of sovereigns,
appoints envoys to them, corresponds with the generals, and
makes the laws.

It seems that each deputy brings to the congress the
vote of his province, and that the decisions of the congress
are then sent to the provinces.

How much soever the subjects of this newborn republic
may be attached to their government, they cannot conceal
from themselves that there are many of those who are
called tories or royalists, who, either from fear or affection, have an attachment for the government of England.

A very large part of the money is of paper, and, unfortunately, it is very much discredited.

Such are the inconveniences, but they vanish when we
remember that, notwithstanding all obstacles, the power
of England has been baffled in America by the love of
country and of liberty, which has hitherto animated the
Anglo-Americans, that many English generals have been
successively defeated there, that Burgoyne has shamefully

passed under the yoke, and that there, more than anywhere else, Voltaire's verses have had their effect, Injustice has finally produced Independence.

Philadelphia was taken by General Howe, who was obliged to abandon it, although supported by his brother, Admiral Howe.

To be well acquainted with this country, we must study the maps, endeavor to know the great rivers, the position of the cities upon the banks of these rivers, from the point to which they are navigable and as far as vessels can ascend.

It would be well to write down all these observations and to begin by an epitome of the revolution; and then to proceed to other observations upon the general administration, that of each province in particular, the laws, the courts, the police, the military forces, the productions, the commerce, etc.; to become well acquainted with the position of the armies, in order to omit nothing that can furnish correct ideas respecting the country and this interesting people.

It should be remembered that great prudence is required in America, when it is necessary to have intercourse with its inhabitants. Especially, should we avoid exhibiting any air of contempt; the people are poor and exhausted by the efforts which they have made to defend their liberty. The French come to assist them, they ought not to display the pride of protection.

JOURNAL.

CHAPTER I.

THE VOYAGE.

Preparations for departure — Composition of the Squadron conveying the auxiliary Forces — Departure from Brest — Voyage — Engagement with an English Squadron at the Bermuda Islands — Considerable number of Deaths and of sick Persons on Board — Another Meeting, without an Engagement, with a Squadron of the Enemy near the Chesapeake Bay — Arrival at Rhode Island and Landing.

The Count De Rochambeau, lieutenant general of the army, having been appointed to command a body of troops, intended to be embarked, without anyone's knowing positively whither they were to proceed, caused me to be employed to serve with these troops as commissary. In consequence, I proceeded to Brest on the 20th of March, 1780.

M. de Tarlé, directing commissary, discharging the functions of intendant to this body of troops, did not arrive there until eight or ten days afterwards; he brought me a commission as chief commissary. Finding myself alone at Brest, I worked with the generals of the land and sea forces in embarking all the goods

1

and supplies needed for the troops after their landing. The navy, being unable to furnish a sufficient number of transports, they were obliged to leave in France the regiments of Neustrie and Anhalt, which were, originally, intended to be embarked, as also two or three hundred men of Lauzun's legion. Only five thousand men were embarked, namely, the regiments of Bourbonnais, Soissonnais, Saintonge, Royal Deux-Ponts, about five hundred artillerists and six hundred men of Lauzun's legion, three hundred of whom were intended to form a troop of horse; these troops, their effects, the artillery and other objects necessary for an army, were embarked in from twenty-five to thirty transports or store-ships; they were escorted by seven ships of war and two frigates, namely :

Ships.	Guns.	Commanders.
The Duke of Burgundy, doubly sheathed with copper,[1]	80	The Chevalier de Ternay, chief of the squadron,
The Neptune, doubly sheathed with copper,	74	Destouches,
The Conquerant,	74	La Grandière,
The Provence,	64	Lombard,

---

[1] Vessels of this class were rare at that day, and were noted for rapid sailing. The admiral hoisted his flag on board of this ship, and General Rochambeau was a passenger, with some of his staff.

Ships.	Guns.	Commanders.
The Eveillé, doubly sheathed with copper,	64	de Tilly,
The Jazon,	64	de Clochetterie,
The Ardent,	64	The Chevalier de Marigny.
Frigates.		
The Surveillante,		Sillart,
The Amazone,		La Perouse,[1]
The Guêpe, a cutter,		The Chevalier de Maulurier.

The Fantasque, an old vessel, was armed *en flute* and was intended to serve as a hospital ; the treasure, the heavy artillery and many passengers were embarked upon it.

All the general officers lay on board on the 14th of April. I was there also and embarked upon the Conquerant. On the first night I lay in the gun room with thirty or forty persons. The next day they prepared a little lodging place for me in the great cabin ; that is where they eat. I lay there in a hammock, in the English fashion, over a cannon. I can write there, sitting on a portmanteau, and I have light through a port-hole.

The convoy started and anchored at Bertheaume, which is likewise in the roadstead, but three leagues

---

[1] The celebrated navigator.

from Brest. On the 16th we were unmoored and ready to follow ; but the wind having changed to the west, we could not raise the anchors : these west winds, which were contrary to us, also lasted for some days. I availed myself of it to go frequently on shore to finish some business which I had been compelled to leave unfinished. Altogether, I was not useless at this embarkation, owing to my activity and concilia-tory disposition. At last, on the 2d of May, the wind changed to the north and we started immmediately. We passed, as did all the convoy, between the Island of the Saints and the Beak of Ratz; this passage is narrow and even dangerous, it is said, but, I believe, not so for good sailors ; we went through without ac-cident. This route took us away from the entrance of the channel and from every undesirable meeting;[1] we made about twenty leagues that day. We would have made more, if the convoy had not obliged us to bring to two or three times : we could not lose sight of them, which often compelled us to wait. The next day, the 3d, we continued our course, by the help of the same north wind, but it was light ; we had almost a dead calm at noon and were only thirty-two leagues from Brest. One of the frigates chased two small ves-

---

[1] The English fleet under Graves was watching for them.

sels. The ships of war and the transports proceeded
in order; on the 4th, we met a Danish ship coming
from Naples and going to Hamburg; we obliged it to
follow us for twenty-four hours. We continued to
sail in this manner in the Gulf of Gascony until the
9th, on which day the wind became directly contrary,
it came from the west; we might then be thirty
leagues from Cape Ortegal. At four o'clock in the
afternoon the wind became violent, it was a real
tempest; we were at the Cape and we remained there
during the whole of the 10th. It is a very painful
situation for persons who suffer from sea-sickness. I
suffered then, and greatly, although I had already
sailed upon the Mediterranean, going to and returning
from Corsica, a voyage which I have often made. I
remained in bed during the whole of the 10th and did
not recover until the 14th. On this day the wind
grew calm and we left the gulf fifteen leagues to the
north west of Cape Finisterre. One of our ships, the
Provence, lost her foretop owing to this bad weather;
the captain wished to leave the squadron, but some
carpenters were sent on board of her and the damage
was quickly repaired. On the 15th, Mons. de Ternay
sent back a frigate which did not form a part of our
squadron; she was to carry news of us and to put into
port in Spain. I was informed of it late, yet I hastily

wrote a word to my wife and to Mons. Coussard. This day and the next, the wind was north and pretty fresh; we made seven knots an hour, which makes two leagues and a third; yet we had only one or two sails hoisted, on account of the convoy, which would not have been able to follow us, and among which there were some laggards. Thus, we lay by every day to give them time to rally. I was now wonderfully well and I profited by it to write the preceding details. Hereafter, I have written every day as will be seen.

May 19*th*. The winds continue northwardly, and although they are not so strong as on the 16th and 17th (on those days we made forty-six leagues[1] in twenty-four hours) we could not be anything else than very well satisfied with the progress which we are making. We were then in the latitude of Cape Vincent, at the distance of about a hundred leagues. Whilst the weather is fine, I am about to write some details respecting the vessel in which I am embarked. At our departure it drew 22 feet of water at the bow, and 19 at the stern; height of the main mast 104 feet; main yard, 95; foresail mast 95 feet; mizzen mast, 74; bowsprit, 62. Here are the names of the naval and military officers, with whom I am embarked.

---

[1] Marine leagues.

La Grandiere, captain,

Chirfontaine, ditto, second in command.

Nupuy, first lieutenant.

Blessing, ditto (a Swedish officer).

Ensigns. La Jonquierès, Kergu, Maccarthy, Duparc de Bellegarde, Buissy.

Naval Guards. Livet, Legritz, Lourmel.

Auxiliary Officers. Cordier, Deshayes, Marassin, Guzence; we left one of them, M. Gautier, sick at Brest.

We also had the captain's son, but he was not yet a marine officer.

Officers of Infantry, a detachment upon the vessel, drawn from the regiment of La Sarre; Laubanie, captain; La Mothe, lieutenant; Loyas, sub-lieutenant.

Passengers. The Baron de Vioménil, major general; Count de Custine, brigadier and colonel of the regiment of Saintonge.

The Grenadier company of the said regiment, of which these were the officers: De Vouves, captain; De James, ditto, in the second class; Champetier, lieutenant; Josselin, lieutenant in the second class; Denis, sub-lieutenant; Fanit, second sub-lieutenant.

Menonville, lieutenant colonel, attached to the staff of the army.

De Chabannes and De Pangé, aides de camp of M. de Vioménil.

Brizon, a cavalry officer, discharging the functions of secretary to the said general.

We also had a surgeon and a chaplain, making part of the staff of the vessel. Including the domestics and the passengers, there are 960 persons on board, with provisions for six months. Up to this day, the 19th, there are no sick on board except several sailors, already attacked by the scurvy at the time of our departure from Brest. However, we have lost an old sailor.

On the 20th, we had the same wind; to-day a man died on board. I remark that we ought not to be surprised that the winds were always from the north or north east. These winds are constant in these parts and are what are called the trade winds. Advantage is taken of them to go to St. Domingo; another route is followed, for returning.

On the 21st, the same wind, and pretty strong; we made 25 leagues in 24 hours. At noon, on the said day, we being in 35° 19′ of latitude, and 20° 19′ of longitude, I ascended to the mizzen-top. I was not lashed there, as is usually done; I gave six livres to the top-men; the first sailors are thus called, those who commonly remain in the tops. To ascend the tops whilst under sail, at about forty years of age, when one is not accustomed to it, is not bad.

On the same day the admiral having signaled to go on board to receive some orders, I accompanied the officer who was sent. M. de Tarlé, our commissary, who had embarked thereon, confirmed me in the belief that we were going to New England and that we would land at Rhode Island. I had always thought that such was our destination, inasmuch as we had embarked goods suitable for the savages, and which must be given to them in the intercourse that we might have with them. They dwell on the frontiers, as is known. I also learnt that a vessel which they had met some days before had mentioned that a Spanish fleet had set out on the 20th of April from Cadiz, but that its destination was unknown.

On the 22d, the same wind, north and north east. We were on the 34th degree of latitude, forty leagues from Madeira, the weather was pretty cloudy this day and, in general, it has always been so since we left Cape Finisterre; we do not experience great heat. This cloudy weather caused me violent head-aches, especially at night, but I experience the same on land. Otherwise, my health was good.

My servant, Bourdais, has been sick for some days with a violent cold and an intermittent fever.

At this period, our real destination was unknown on board, and many persons supposed that we were

going to Jamaica. They believed it the rather because, for reasons which I shall explain hereafter, we
bore much towards the south, and were following
the route which is taken to go to Jamaica or Saint
Domingo.

The 25th, Corpus Christi day. The latitude, 35°.
We continued to make from 25 to 30 leagues a day,
the convoy preventing our doing more : every day we
lay to.

The Isle of France, a store-ship, or, at least, a large
transport ship, which had a part of the regiment of
Bourbonnais on board, and wherein my brother-in-law
was the Chevalier de Coriolis, a lieutenant in this regiment, had taken in tow the *Baron d'Arras*, another
transport ship. On the same day, a vessel armed as
a man of war and laden with merchandise, called the
Lutin, which had followed us up to this day, left us
to proceed to Cayenne.

I remark that on the 24th the admiral had slightly
altered his course and borne more towards the west ;
nevertheless the reasoners considered that we were
still going too far towards the south.

For some days past we have seen in the wake of
the vessel, a great number of fishes which they said
were bormites ; the crew took one of them weighing
four pounds ; this fish tastes like the tunny-fish, but

it seemed to me not so good and drier. In the Mediterranean they are called polominé.

Sunday the 27th at noon we were in latitude 29° 55′ and had made 30 leagues in our 24 hours. Our politicians are still in a state of uncertainty, seeing us go so much to the south, and there are some who pretend that we are going to Porto Rico to take some Spaniards. Notwithstanding all my presumptions for believing that we were going to North America, I myself will soon no longer know what to think of it.

On the 28th, at noon, the admiral signaled the point of the compass and to bear towards the west; then all doubts were dispelled, and we saw plainly that we were going to New England. I made a bet, this day, that we would see the coast on the 26th of June, and persisted in asserting that we would land upon Rhode Island.

We were in the latitude of 28° and as high up as the Azores at the moment when the point of the compass was signaled.

It appears that this route, so much to the south, had been directed by the court in order to avoid the English : it is the same which M. d'Estaing followed in 1778, and which we verified by the diary of M. de Bellegarde, an ensign on board of our vessel, who had been in M. d'Estaing's squadron. We bore towards

the west, exactly in the same latitude as he. Some
sailors pretend that the northern route is preferable ;
it is much shorter ; yet Admiral Byron, who followed
it when he was running after M. d'Estaing, was greatly
delayed therein and arrived after the French admiral.
After all, this route enabled us to avoid the English,
whom we must especially avoid on account of the
convoy.

The 29th. According to the pilot's report, we have
made 36 leagues, and it seems that we continue to go
along well ; for the wind is fresh and directly from
the east, which gives us a wind in our stern, as we
proceed westwardly. We have few sick persons ; my
servant is better. As to myself, at the moment when
I am writing, I am perfectly well and without any
indisposition, not the least head ache ; I cannot say
as much concerning the preceding days, having been
tormented by it almost continually. Without doubt
these head aches proceed from the stomach, owing to
the bad food on board.[1] Tea has been very beneficial

---

[1] Let me be pardoned for recurring so often to my health ; it
proves that when one is on board ship, he has little diversion
and concerns himself much about himself. I ought also to say
that I had scarcely recovered from illness when I went to sea.
This sickness, which I had neglected, I had contracted at Mor-
tain, whither I was called, during the autumn of 1779, to put in
order the hospitals of that city, crowded with 2000 patients,

13

to me in these head aches, especially if a little citron was put therein. I write these details for my children and friends, who may be obliged to go to sea. At sea, if one suffers, he is disgusted, disheartened and curses the sea, but these moments pass away and one loves it. I perceived that I should become accustomed to it and that this service would even have been attractive to me. Whilst I am writing, I feel happy; it is true that we have reason to be satisfied with all the officers, excepting the captain, who is ill-humored, devout, illiberal, selfish, communing every Sunday; without being more humane towards the sailors and the sick, in short announcing a Molinist religion.

On the 31st,[1] we discovered at noon that we had

---

proceeding from the squadron of M. Voirilliers, which had returned to Brest a short time before. These patients, attacked by dysentery and putrid fever were massed in five hospitals, hastily established ; I there lost a large part of the nurses and many surgeons and apothecaries. The only two physicians who were charged with the care of these five hospitals, contracted serious diseases there, of which they nearly died. As I did not spare myself on this occasion, I suffered from this pestilence for a long time, the rather as I took no preventive. I may say that the labors which I then underwent were not ignored, and that I procured myself some honor. [An interesting note and a sad picture of the old French military administration, and which does not seem to have improved in these latter days.]

[1] I do not find any remark upon the 30th, and I suspect that some mistake as to the date has crept into my journal since the 26th and 27th when I was sick ; there is also a date erased.

made 41 leagues; I observe that it is always at noon that the pilot marks the point where we are upon the chart, and that he gives the longitude and the latitude to the captain of the vessel, since it is at noon that he ascertains the last and takes the altitude; it is at noon also that a report is made of the progress that has been made since noon on the day before : therefore when I say that we have gone 20 or 30 leagues it is always since noon on the preceding day.

June. This day, the first of June, we saw much sea-weed [goëmon] ; we began to see it at the 30th degree of latitude, and this continues as far as the tropics. The grape of the tropics is also called goëmon.

The goëmon is a grass which is detached from the submarine rocks and from the Canary islands; it has small grains shaped like grapes; the sea is entirely covered with it.

On the 2d, we sent on board the admiral's ship : there it was openly said that we were about to land at Newport in the island of Rhode Island. At noon, I desired to take the altitude myself. I was struck by seeing the sun directly over our heads ; I had not paid attention to it up to that moment.

On the 3d, the wind being light, we made only 18 leagues. This day, the captains of the ships of the line were ordered to go on board of the admiral's ship, who probably gave them some instructions concerning making land.

On the 4th, little wind still, we made only 17 leagues. A negro sailor died on boaid of our ship. We then had about sixty sick persons in the Conquerant. The other vessels had much fewer, but it must be observed that the Conquerant had been fitted out for a long time, that it had left Brest on the 22d of February with M. de Guichen, but that having sustained damage it was compelled to return : the whole crew was composed of men, both sailors and soldiers, who had been at sea for a long time. The other vessels had just been fitted out at the time of our departure, and the crews were men who, for the most part, had arrived from their own homes. We also had on board about 150 persons more than the usual number on a vessel of our size, which occasioned crowding and was injurious to the wholesomeness of the air. Besides it seems to me that little attention was paid to the health of the crew and that the sick were neglected.

On the 5th, we made only 5 leagues; we took a gold fish, a fish which has beautiful colors and is very good to eat.

On the 6th, we chased five vessels in the morning, but we could not discover what they were ; as they would have drawn us too much out of our course if we had continued to follow them much longer, the admiral caused the chase to cease. It seems to me that it would, nevertheless, have been interesting to ascertain what they were in order to obtain news; besides, they might have been English vessels coming from India, and that would have been a good prize : that was their course for returning to Europe, for they usually follow that latitude to reach the Azores. We were then in the latitude of 27° 31' and the longitude of 43° 39'. The admiral signaled a change of course or point of the compass and we ran west a quarter north west and, consequently, we were to proceed no farther south.

On the 7th, the heat was powerful, the sky clear and cloudless.

On the 8th, the admiral signaled a change of the point of the compass and bore due west.

On the 9th, the wind is cool. We lost three men, two of whom were soldiers ; one died the evening before ; eight in all since our departure.

On the 11th, M. de Viomenil and M. de Custine received the order of battle, or instructions respecting our landing and some other details concerning our expedition.

On the 12th, at 6 o'clock in the morning, our frigates which had been ordered the night before to chase a little vessel, brought it with them; it was English and laden with codfish; it was coming from Halifax and was bound to St. Eustacia. It told us that a vessel of Arbuthnot's squadron, called the Defiance, had been lost on the coast of New England, that the Robust, a ship of war of the same squadron, had also been greatly damaged and compelled to return to Halifax; it also informed us that M. de Guichen arrived at Martinico on the 29th of March, and that Rodney had not yet appeared there on the 6th of April. We also learnt that the English were still busy in Carolina, but that Charleston was not taken. The admiral caused the codfish and the herrings with which this little vessel was laden to be divided among the ships of war of the squadron, and, after having pillaged and unrigged it, we abandoned it. This day we made 30 leagues.

On the 13th, the admiral slightly changed his course and bore more towards the west. Without doubt, he was unwilling to go near the Bermudas, where gales of wind are always encountered, and where we might also meet with some English ships, which it was essential to avoid, having a convoy and assistance so important to convey to the Americans.

The 14th, remarkably cool; the admiral caused the squadron to advance, for some time, in order of battle, that is to say, in a single line; we usually proceeded in two, and even in three, the *flutes* forming one line. The remainder of the convoy kept to the windward of the squadron. To-day I saw a flying-fish. They had been seen for some days past; these fishes are one or two feet long; they rather leap than fly, and it is their fins that support them. That which I saw kept himself between wind and water; he passed over about five or six fathoms. A soldier of the regiment of La Sarre died on board.

On the 16th, we calculated that we were only two hundred leagues from St. Domingo, where we would. have been already if that had been our destination. The heat was powerful, we were 4° from the tropic and were approaching the moment when the sun turns (June 21st) ; consequently, it was almost perpendicular over our heads. So far, our voyage is agreeable, hardly any heavy sea, a good wind, no accident and few annoyances. Our ship was the only one suffering from sickness. To-day another man died.

On the 18th, we found ourselves in the longitude of the Bermudas ; it is this high up that the trade winds cease and that variable winds are found. At 9 o'clock a vessel was signaled, at 10 o'clock it was joined by our frigates, which it waited for, supposing that it was an English squadron that it perceived. This vessel, which was an English brig, had fourteen four-pounders and some swivels; it had left Charleston at the beginning of the month and was going to Barbadoes to transport five officers who were rejoining their regiments, and to carry some dispatches of the British minister; it had only a crew of thirty men; they gave us four sailors on board of the Conquerant. We learnt from this vessel that the city of Charleston had surrendered to the English on the 4th of May, and that the siege began on the 1st of April. These news made us desire more than ever to reach Newport or some other point which the Americans should point out to us. They also told us of an engagement between Rodney and M. de Guichen, but in a confused manner, and without telling us of the result.

On the 19th, we sent ten sick persons on board of the *Fantasque;* we had already sent as many to it some days before. This vessel was intended to serve as a hospital, although having several passengers on board.

On the 20th, we had made 34 leagues. At noon the admiral signaled to steer to the north-west; we were then in 30° 24′ of latitude and 69° 20′ of longitude. At half after one sails were signaled, which we caused to be reconnoitered by the *Neptune* and the *Eveillé*, our best sailers. These sails bore down upon us; we did not delay in approaching them. At 4 o'clock the

Neptune signaled that it was a hostile squadron ; it was then very near one of the vessels of this squadron and we supposed that it was about to commence the engagement, which we would have supported, seeing that we followed the *Neptune* pretty closely. Every one on board of us was at his post, and the beating to quarters had been ordered and executed. Then the admiral gave the signal for forming in line of battle, and we ran upon the same tack as the enemy, who were then bearing to the south-west. It required some time to form in line, because the vessels had chased without regard to order, and each of them had to regain its post. It was said that the admiral ought to have formed the line without regard to rank. However that may be, we then perceived very distinctly five ships of war and a frigate : three seemed to us to be of 74 guns. At five o'clock the chaplain gave us the benediction ; I visited all the posts with the Baron Vioménil ; everywhere we witnessed the greatest gaiety and the best behavior. The English were to the windward, and our convoy, well collected, were to the leeward of us. One of the enemy's vessels seemed to wish to throw itself alongside of our convoy; it was the first of the English line ; we supposed it to be cut off by the Neptune, which was also at the head of our line. But the admiral, who wished to preserve

his line and cover his convoy, ordered it to slacken
sail, which was done. The Englishman then tried to
rejoin his squadron. It was six o'clock in the evening,
we then displayed the French flag, the English hoisted
that of their nation ; and immediately the Neptune
and the English ship, which was in advance of its line,
began to cannonade each other, and in succession all
our ships fired. The English vessel, against which
the Neptune had fought, manœuvred very well and returned to take the tail of its line ; it was exposed to
all the fire of ours, whilst replying. We fought a
little too far from each other. The English, who were
to the windward, might have come nearer, but they
did not seem to care about it. Nevertheless we saw
very distinctly some of our shot reach the English
vessels ; our ships for their part also received some.
As to our ship, it did not appear to have received a
single ball; the English fired *too high,* for we heard
the balls passing over our heads. This cannonade
lasted about a quarter of an hour. During this time,
I was before the mast with M. de Vioménil ; we also
proceeded back of the mast near the captain, and once
or twice I ascended the quarter deck bunk to understand the manœuvres better. The admiral, after this
first cannonade, gave the signal to take by counter-
marching, desiring by that means to get near the
enemy : as we formed the rear guard and as we were

the last to perform this movement, we greatly enjoyed
the sight of this manœuvre, which is very handsome
and which was very well executed. The English
made no move in opposition to it and then showed that
they were unwilling to prolong this engagement; it
was seven o'clock in the evening. Our ships again
fired some broadsides, especially at the vessel of the
rear guard, which had already been exposed to the
whole fire of our line. It replied on its part and did
not cease firing. As to us, it appeared to us too distant, and we despised firing upon it to no purpose.
The sun was about to set and the English withdrew.
It was too late to follow them; besides it would have
been useless, they seemed to be good sailers and we
had bad sailers. Besides, the convoy, of which it
would have been imprudent to lose sight, would ne-
cessarily have delayed us. During the whole time the
wind had been southwardly, it was a little cool, the
sea was fine and everything was favorable for joining
battle or being a spectator of it. This was not such
as it might be; but it might become murderous. We
had the beginning of it. It is then that one may
judge of the behavior of a person in it. They were
satisfied with mine, and I was satisfied with it
myself. In general every one conducted himself
well, and the captain set us the example of it. I

have not given a handsome portrait of him ; but we pardon his defects on a day of battle, then he exhibited much activity and great composure. I am writing to-day, the 21st of June, the details of this encounter according to the impression made upon me, and such as I have beheld it ; and I believe that M. de Ternay could not have behaved otherwise than he did, as well on account of the convoy as with respect to the little daylight which was left when the English retired. Notwithstanding, from that very day I have heard him blamed by some naval officers and other persons, sufficiently enlightened : first, for having formed his line according to the order of battle ; secondly, for having signaled the Neptune to slacken sail at the moment when it was about to cut off the English ship with which it was engaged, and which would have been undoubtedly captured, as they allege ; or else the English would have desired to assist it, which would have brought on the engagement, which must have been to our advantage, since we had two more vessels, were better armed and had captains of ships truly distinguished for their courage, such as M. de la Clochetterie and M. de Marigny. I shall not undertake to decide this question ; moreover, I shall return to this cannonade and shall insert in my journal the details which will be drawn up respecting it by some man in the service, contenting myself in these first moments with mentioning in my own way what I have seen and what I think. The English having disappeared, we proceeded in a bow and quarter line, steering to the north-west. On the evening of the engagement, whilst conversing with the *Ardent*, by means of a speaking-trumpet we learnt that the *Neptune* had had two men killed and five or six wounded.

On the 21st, at noon, we found that we had made 21 leagues, notwithstanding the time which we had lost owing to this encounter; we saw the English no more, but we captured a small vessel belonging to that nation, laden with sailors going from Savannah to Jamaica. That day we lost two men, a soldier and a negro servant. All the sick whom we had shut up during the fight in the holds, had suffered greatly, many had come up on the deck and had taken their posts. This soldier who died had asked the favor of being allowed to serve. This day the admiral caused the captain to come on board of his vessel; we learnt that the *Duke of Burgundy* had had two men killed and five or six wounded, and in the whole squadron they summed up 21 men killed or wounded. It was suspected on board of the *Duke of Burgundy* that it was Admiral Arbuthnot whom we had met, and that he was proceeding to Jamaica; that was also our

opinion, which agreed with that of the English officers who were prisoners in our ships.

On the 22d, 22 leagues. In the evening we had a
dead calm. I took advantage of it to go on board of
the *Ardent,* to see my comrade, M. de Villemanzy, who
was on board of it, and M. Demars, the manager of
the hospitals. It seemed to me that they greatly regretted there that we had not come nearer to the
enemy. M. de Marigny, without explaining himself
too much, seemed to regret it more than any one else ;
an answer of his to the admiral was quoted, which
deserves to be related ; the latter asked him with
what English admiral he believed that they had been
engaged. M. de Marigny replied : " We have lost the
opportunity of finding it out." To-day, several sails
were perceived from the tops of the masts ; six of
them were counted, which were presumed to be the
ships which we had fought.

On the 23d, in the morning, the calm ended : the
wind was from the west and we may have made 14
leagues by noon. We went on a direct course towards
Rhode Island, from which we were distant 160 leagues.
The nearest land might be distant 110 leagues. Some
vessels were perceived which were chased to no purpose. The *Guépe* entered into this pursuit so far that

4

we lost sight of her; she did not rejoin the squadron until very late at night.

On the 24th, 15 leagues; in the evening, we again had almost a dead calm. M. de Viomenil's brother, who was on board of the *Neptune*, came aboard of our ship. According to what he said to us, it did not appear that they were as much dissatisfied aboard of the *Neptune* with M. de Ternay's conduct as upon the other ships. They only thought on board of this ship that he might, without inconvenience, have permitted it to chase the enemy's ship which it was pursuing, and which it had attacked, as I have related; it was a ship of 64 guns. They had lost only one man by sickness on board of the Neptune, and they had not the scurvy there; we have already seen that we were not in so good a condition, very far from it.

Note added, on copying this journal:

If I have spoken of this combat at great length, it is because it interests me much and also because we are incessantly speaking of it among ourselves. On a vessel, the least event occupies the mind, and especially those of this sort. To-day when I am cool, I judge without passion and with more experience: I will therefore confess that I have defended M. de Ternay too much. It is certain that his chief object being to carry assistance to the Americans, he ought not to risk an engagement so lightly, nor rashly to expose the generals of the land forces and the troops which are on board of the ships of war; but on this occasion he had so decided a superiority that he was really wrong in causing the *Neptune* to slacken sail or in forming his line in such a way as caused him to lose much time.

Besides, we have since learnt that the five vessels were commanded by Commodore Cornwallis, who was returning to Europe with them after having escorted a convoy, which was returning to Europe, as high up as the Bermudas. The account that he has given of this engagement is not entirely correct. It is to be found in the *Gazette of Utrecht* of October 27th, 1780, and the *Courier of Europe* of the 13th of the same month. He states that only three men were killed and five wounded in his squadron, which seems impossible, cne of his ships having been twice exposed to the fire of our whole squadron. Our ships, which received the fire of only a single English vessel, had many more.

Here is the list of this English squadron over which we had a great superiority of force.

The Bristol, 50 guns; The Sultan, 74; The Lion, 64; on board of which was the commodore. The Hector, 74, and the Ruby, 64. (This is the one that was engaged). He also had one frigate.

The 25th, 15 leagues.

The 26th, 16 leagues. A soldier of the regiment of La Sarre, who had the scurvy, died on board.

The 27th, 27 leagues. In the evening, the wind became violent and changeable; there was thunder and the admiral made us lie to; we remained there all night. The sea was rough. We lost a sailor.

On the 28th, at 10 o'clock, the sea became calmer. At noon, we had made 13 leagues. We were then in latitude 35° 45′ and in longitude 74° 24′. The general signaled a course to the west-north-west, which led us towards Chesapeake bay. We again lost a man. On the 30th, another.

On the first of July the wind was from the northeast. According to the pilot's observations, we were in the latitude of Chesapeake bay and we had run less to the north than we had supposed, which proves that there are currents. We saw plainly that we had been deceived in the calculation of our longitudes, for, according to those which the pilot had given us, we ought to be in Chesapeake bay, and it seems that we were still far from it; for not only were we unable to see the land, but on sounding we found no bottom. Another soldier who had the scurvy died.

On the 2d of July, 15 leagues; we still bore towards Chesapeake bay. In the evening we were becalmed.

On the 3d, the wind rose. They again sounded without finding bottom ; we were all very impatient to see land ; our voyage was beginning to be long, and we had a great number of sick persons on board. The scurvy was seizing the whole crew, and even the company of Grenadiers of Saintonge. We were the more impatient to arrive as, according to all the observations of the pilot of the squadron on the longitudes, we ought to have arrived already. However, these mistakes in longitudes are common, and there is no sure method of rectifying them ; well-regulated chronometers may give some pretty nearly, but this method has not been sufficiently tried.

Besides, the watches which were on board of the Duke of Burgundy had not been well regulated on our departure. I observe also that a squadron which often lies to, which increases or slackens sail at every moment, is more likely to be deceived in the reckoning of its longitudes than a vessel which goes alone and uniformly ; it may also be that our charts are not exact, and that New England is improperly put down upon them.

On the 4th, a sailor died; we lost one of them the night before. I learnt it from the surgeon-major with whom I was intimately acquainted ; for otherwise these events would not be known in the round house where we remain, nor even upon deck. A dead man is thrown into the sea through a port-hole, and no one sees it except the persons entrusted with the care of the sick, who are kept in the lowest parts of the ship. On the same day the pilot gave us only 27 leagues. At one o'clock we paid out as much as eight knots, which makes three leagues, less one-third. A small vessel was discovered which our frigates chased. It discharged its guns two or three times, but after a chase of two hours it surrendered. Whilst the Amazone was lashing it, the Surveillante signaled that it had found bottom at 22 fathoms, which has occasioned great joy and gave us hope of seeing land to-day. I am writing this a moment afterwards. The Conquerant has also just sounded ; it found 25 fathoms. The admiral has made us lie to. We learnt from the Amazone, on board of which we sent, that the prize which we have just taken was coming from New York and was going to Charleston ; it was a merchantman laden with wine ; it confirmed us in the opinion that we were only eight or nine leagues from shore and from the entrance of Chesapeake bay. At half after four, we resumed our course, and at six o'clock we could not be more than five or six leagues from land. The admiral having perceived some sails in front of us and in the direction of the land, which was not in sight, and believing that they were large vessels, he gave the signal to clear the decks for action and then to tack about, so that we went away from the land. It was suspected that the vessels which we saw were those which Admiral Graves was bringing from Europe, and among which were some with three decks. We expected to be pursued and attacked during the night; but at daybreak we saw only two vessels which seemed to be frigates; one of them bore the English flag; our admiral chased them with two frigates. It was about six o'clock when this chase began; at ten o'clock the admiral ordered it to be discontinued, as he perceived that the vessels in pursuit were not gaining upon the enemy's vessels. This was unfortunate; for besides that they might have afforded us some useful information, such a prize would have delighted us; we had to regret removing from the land, only five or six leagues distant, in order to go now in search of it at a greater distance. At three o'clock we lay to in order to collect the convoy, which was scattered. The admiral restored order. We learnt by the return of the officer of our ship that the two vessels which had been chased had been mingled with us during the night and had even discharged their cannons twice at the Duke of Burgundy and the Neptune; it was fortunate that they had not fastened upon the convoy; they might

have captured some vessel or at least have damaged
it. According to appearances, their design was to
have themselves chased and to entice one or two of
our vessels into the midst of the English squadron,
which, doubtless, was not so strong as had been supposed, since it did not pursue us. The officers of our
frigates say that they were gaining upon the English
vessels, one of which was of 26 guns and the other
only a corvette of 18 ; they offered in proof that one
of these frigates had itself admitted that we had the
advantage over it, since it had thrown its boat and its
spare maintop mast into the sea, in order to lighten it.
The admiral continued his course towards Rhode Island ; yet he said that circumstances might induce
him to proceed to Boston ; he also declared that he
had never intended to enter Chesapeake bay, except
to procure water and to land his sick ; that it had always been his intention to land the army at Newport
or Boston. This assertion of his was disbelieved by
many ; and he was blamed for having tacked about on
the evening of the 4th, when he perceived some vessels ; we ought to have gone near to ascertain pre-
cisely their number and strength. Not more than
eight had ever been counted, among which there had,
perhaps, been some frigates. If it was too late on that
day, the 4th, when these sails were perceived, we might

have lain to, after coming as near as possible, and have rejoined them at daybreak. These reflections did not escape the crews, thus they were dissatisfied and lost confidence in their leader; it was, therefore, greatly to be desired that they should land speedily and not meet the enemy's squadron, and the rather as we had two hundred and fifty sick.

Note. It is certain that M. de Ternay manœuvred very badly on this occasion. I have heard this asserted by M. de Cappellis, a very well-informed naval officer, who was attached to the admiral on board of the Duke of Burgundy. He manœuvred so much the worse, as we have learnt that these vessels were only a convoy, escorted by only two or three ships of war, and that the frigates which mixed themselves among us had been sent to take up our time *and to draw us away. They risked them to save the convoy.* However, it has been more to our advantage that we landed in Rhode Island instead of Chesapeake bay; it is cooler; the air there is much more healthful; the army and the squadron recovered there much better and more rapidly.

On the 6th, at noon, we had made 24 leagues; we were in the latitude of 38° and longitude of 75°; the wind was favorable, the sea calm. We saw many

5

sharks and porpoises or blowers; some were more than 25 feet long.

On the 7th, 25 leagues. We lost a man. It is supposed that we are not more than 50 leagues from Newport. The captains of the ships were summoned. I accompanied M. de la Grandiere and learnt that we were positively to proceed to Newport and not to Boston. It had been foggy all day, in the evening it became very thick and the ships could not see each other; therefore, that they might not run foul of each other, cannons and muskets were fired from time to time; this fog lasted all night.

On the 8th, in the morning, the fog cleared off, but we had calms, so that at noon we had made only 12 leagues. Again we lost a sailor. In the afternoon, the fog reappeared, we did not perceive a single vessel. This fog lasted all night and was accompanied by thunder. These fogs are very frequent in these seas and as far as the banks of Newfoundland; it also happens that a troubled sea is found there without there being any wind; this proceeds from the banks of sand; as we approach them that is produced which is called the *accords* of a bank, and the sea is always rough.

At this period and for about a month past, notwithstanding the bad food, especially the bad water, and the scurvy, by which we were surrounded, I was very well ; in speaking of the water, I will say that although it was black and unpleasant to the sight, it had not a bad taste ; we had drunk some of it which had been on board for six months.

On the 9th, in the morning, one of our frigates sounded and found bottom at forty fathoms.

The fog became thicker than it had yet been. At half after 11, being about three leagues from Block island, a little island situated four leagues from Rhode island, the admiral by eight discharges of cannon, gave a signal for anchoring, which was done. The wind was cool and the fog very thick ; yet this manœuvre was very successful and without accident. I am writing this a moment afterwards, about noon. It is very desirable that the fog should cease and that we should at least be able to land. The condition of our sick is worse, and *a battle would not be more murderous than a longer stay at sea.* We are in a very critical moment. Shall we meet the English before landing, and will they have a superior force ? At any rate, it is to their interest to attack us. Therefore the general opinion is that we shall not land without firing a gun, and perhaps at the moment when we least expect it. An English squadron may be near us without our knowing it on account of the fog. *How shall we be re-*

ceived by the Americans? Have they not made their peace? or, at least, have not the English seized the ground to which we expect to proceed? These are the questions which we ask each other. I have, therefore, reason to say that we are in a critical and truly interesting situation; and it is to be regretted that we have not met with any American vessel; it is still more surprising that they have not sent any one to meet us.

At half after one, the fog began to disperse; then the admiral signaled to raise the anchor and to set sail. We found ourselves very near him and conversed with M. de Rochambeau; he invited M. de Vioménil to go and talk with him. He did so and, on his return, told us that M. de Ternay's intention was to go as near to the land as possible and then, if we did not meet with the enemy, to land M. de Rochambeau and his staff; that, for this purpose, he would go on board of a frigate and, as soon as he has gone, a signal will be made on board of the Duc de Bourgogne for M. de Vioménil's going to it with me, that he may take command of the troops which are not landed, and that I may receive his orders respecting the business of my department; M. de Tarlé, the directing commissary, is to accompany M. de Rochambeau. At half past three on the same day we set sail. A minute afterwards one of the merchantmen which we had captured signaled the land. At four o'clock, it was discovered from the masts of our vessel; at five o'clock, we all saw it very distinctly: After a voyage of 69 days, this was a great joy; our sick people came out of their beds, and this sight seemed to restore them to health. I am writing in the first moment of excitement; one should have been at sea, in the midst of the sick and dying, to feel it thoroughly. What adds to our satisfaction is that we do not discover a sail, and that, according to appearance, we shall land without hindrance, which is greatly to be desired, I repeat it, for there are many sick, not only on our vessel but upon all those of the squadron and of the convoy. On the same day at about eight o'clock, the admiral made us anchor; we were three leagues from the land; what we saw was Martha's Vineyard, a little island lying to the north and twelve leagues from Rhode island. We again lost two sailors.

On the 10th, at four o'clock in the morning, the admiral caused us to set sail; towards noon, some pilots reached us from the neighboring islands. The one whom we had on board told us that the Americans were still masters of Rhode Island and that he did not believe that the English had a greater force than ours in these seas. This man was from the island of

Martha's Vineyard ; he had come of his own accord to offer us his services ; he was a good man and displayed intelligence. He was neither a royalist nor *insurgent*, but a friend to everybody, as he told us with much simplicity. At ten o'clock in the evening, we anchored. Another sailor died.

On the 11th, at four o'clock in the morning, we raised the anchor. At seven o'clock, during foggy weather, a vessel of the convoy gave a signal of danger; it was very near the land ; before long, we perceived it ourselves. The admiral made us anchor, the rather as the fog was growing thicker : but it soon dispersed at eight o'clock ; we saw the land very distinctly, which was on one side, Point Judith, from which we were only a league distant, and on the other, Rhode island. We distinguished the shore of Point Judith perfectly well ; it appeared pleasant to us. But what we saw with great satisfaction was a French flag placed upon each of the two shores which were in front of us. This signal, doubtless agreed upon with M. de La Fayette, who had preceded our squadron, informed us that the English were not masters of Rhode island, and that we would be well received there. M. de Rochambeau and the officers of his staff repaired on board of the Amazone, which immediately set sail for Newport, where he arrived before noon. For my part, I went with M. de Vioménil on board of the Duc de Bourgogne, as had been agreed upon.

In the meanwhile, the vessels of the convoy raised their anchors and also proceeded to Newport. The wind was light, but having risen at four o'clock, M. de Ternay caused the ships of war to set sail; the sea was calm and everything favored our progress so that we reached Newport about seven o'clock. The ships anchored pretty near each other a quarter of a league from the city. M. de La Touche, a naval lieutenant, the commander of the frigate Hermione, who had left Rochefort a month before us, to announce our arrival and to conduct M. de La Fayette as well as M. de Corny, came on board of the Duc de Burgogne and confirmed what we had already learnt from our pilots, that he had had an engagement a short time before with an English frigate of equal force, an engagement which had been nearly equal on both sides, and in which he had 10 men killed and 37 wounded; he himself had received a ball in his arm. The Englishman had lost more men, but had been less damaged in the rigging.

Note. When M. de La Fayette set out for America, it was a question whether a commissary should be given to him, in order to prepare what would be necessary for our troops. They cast their eyes upon me; but I was at Nantes, and although it was proposed to

send a courier to me, they calculated that I would not
have twenty-four hours to prepare for my departure.
M. de Corny was then appointed, who did not belong
to the expedition, and who happened to be at Ver-
sailles ; it occasioned great expense and was not of
much assistance.   I will speak of it again.

CHAPTER II.

Landing at Rhode Island — Threatened Attack of an English Fleet — Establishment of the Hospitals — M. Blanchard is sent to Boston — Rhode Island is placed in a State of Defense — Composition of the Army — First Intercourse of the French Generals with General Washington — Residence at Providence — Its Environs — Markets for the Army — Winter Quarters of the French Forces.

(From July 12th, 1780 to March 27th, 1781.)

On the 12th of July, 1780, the day after our arrival, the troops had not yet landed; there was even an express prohibition against landing, and I did not obtain permission until four o'clock in the afternoon. I, therefore, placed my foot upon the earth at Newport. This city is small, but handsome; the streets are straight and the houses, although mostly of wood, of agreeable shape. In the evening there was an illumination. I entered the house of an inhabitant, who received me very well; I took tea there, which was served by a young lady.

On the 13th, I was at Papisquash on the main land, twenty leagues from Newport, to examine an

6

establishment which M. de Corny had arranged for our sick. I stopped at Bristol, a village not far from Papisquash, and looked for an inn where I might dine; but I found nothing there but coffee and badly-raised bread; we were obliged to have it toasted to be able to eat it. I was with M. Demars, the steward of the hospitals, and M. Corte, the first physician. We were obliged to pay 12 livres for the passage of a ferry-boat : they asked 30 of us : we found on our way some pretty houses; but the country is generally barren in the part which we traversed; there are few trees and they are not very hardy. From this day, the 13th, our troops began to disembark.

On the 14th and 15th the troops finished landing and encamping about half a league from Newport. We sent some of the sick to Papisquash, and, at the same time, put some of them in an establishment hastily formed at Newport. On the 15th, the frigate Hermione, which M. de Ternay sent to cruise from the instant of our arrival, to go in search of the Isle of France, one of our transports which had become separated from us during the fogs of which I have spoken, returned without having found it. This transport was conveying 350 men of the regiment of Bourbonnois, some military stores, and many effects belonging to the general officers; we

were all very uneasy, and I more than any one
else : my brother-in-law, *the Chevalier de Coriolis*,
an officer of the regiment of Bourbonnois, was on
board of it.[1] Nevertheless, we hoped that this vessel might reach Boston, and we impatiently waited
for news of it.

On the 16th, we sent a great number of the sick to
Papisquash. For this purpose, I was in the harbor on
board of several vessels. On the same day I went to
occupy a lodging that was furnished in a very pretty
house ; previously, I had lodged with M. de Tarlé ; I
also continued to live with him.

On the 17th, in the morning, I chanced to enter a
school. The master seemed to me a very worthy
man ; he was teaching some children of both sexes ;
all were neatly clad ; the room in which the school
was kept was also very clean. I saw the writing of
these children, it appeared to me to be handsome,
among others, that of a young girl 9 or 10 years old,
very pretty and very modest and such as I would like
my own daughter to be, when she is as old ; she was
called *Abigail Earl*, as I perceived upon her copy-book,
on which her name was written. I wrote it myself, adding to it " very pretty."[2] This school had really in-

---

[1] Batistaine de Coriolis.
[2] These two words are in English in the original.

terested me, and the master had not the air of a missionary but the tone of the father of a family.

On the 18th, I visited, in company with M. de Rochambeau, an Anabaptist temple,[1] where we established a hospital.

On the 19th, I was at Papisquash, where there were already 280 sick persons; but they were far from being provided with everything that was necessary for them; fortunately, they were in a pretty good air. Papisquash forms a kind of landscape surrounded by trees. The commonest are acacias, pear-trees and cherry-trees; the ground is sown with flax and maize, with a little barley and rye. Besides, our sick who had the scurvy began to recover; vegetables were furnished them and the physician allowed them to eat cherries. We lived on good terms with the inhabitants of this neighborhood. They are affable, well clad, very cleanly and all tall. The women enjoy the same advantages, have fair skins and are generally pretty. They all have oxen and cows, at least as handsome as those of our Poitou; their cows are not stabled and pass the night in the fields; they give much milk.

On the 20th I returned to Newport; I there learnt that the Isle of France had put into port at Boston,

---

[1] Protestant churches are called *temples* in France.

which was very good news for me, as for everyone
else.

On the 21st, after having dined with the Baron de
Vioménil, as we were at the quarters of General de
Rochambeau, who was holding a council, we were informed that several vessels were perceived steering for
Newport; it was four o'clock; he immediately mounted
his horse and caused several batteries to be established
upon the shore. M. de Ternay, for his part, made
some arrangements. The vessels that were discovered.
were lying to at nightfall. I also mounted on horseback and saw them very plainly; I counted nineteen
of them.

On the 22d, the same vessels still appeared, they
cruised all day; it was not likely that they would attempt to enter Newport. M. de Rochambeau, with
whom I dined that day, said publicly that he wished
that the English would attempt it. At this dinner
were several Americans, all good patriots, and also an
English officer, who was a prisoner. They addressed
some sharp words to each other; which proves how
earnest both parties were.

On the 23d, we still saw the English; there were
eleven large vessels, the rest were frigates or transports. M. de Rochambeau came to hear mass at the
hospital and to visit the sick; we had 400 of them at

Newport and 280 at Papisquash ; the detachment of
the regiment of Bourbonnois, which had landed at
Boston, also had a hundred of them, so that we had
about 800 sick out of a body of troops amounting to
5000 men ; for I speak only of the sick among the land
forces. The navy had its own in its own hospitals.
The royal regiment of Deux-Ponts had 300 of them ; it
appears that the Germans feel the heat more and are
more subject to the scurvy than the French. All
these maladies had begun to manifest themselves when
we were in the latitude of 27°. There is reason to believe that we shall save many of them ; the air of
Rhode Island is good ; it is hot there, but only in the
middle of the day ; for the mornings and evenings are
cool without being damp. I have not been able to ascertain positively the degree of heat, not having a
thermometer. At present, the temperature seems to
me to be the same as that of the island of Corsica, 24°
on an average.

On the 24th, the detachment of the regiment of
Bourbonnois, which had landed at Boston, arrived at
Newport. I saw my brother-in-law, to whom I gave
a dinner the next day.

On the 25th, it was decided that I should go to Boston to introduce a little order into the hospital which
had been hastily established there to receive the sick

who had been landed from the Isle of France. In the evening the Count de Rochambeau sent me some letters to carry to the captain of a French vessel which was at Boston, and which was expected to sail immediately. The general sent for me again and pretty late, since I had gone to bed. I went to him; he asked me to start on horseback the next day, as early as possible (I was to go in a coach with M. de Capellis, a naval officer) and he gave me some letters for the Boston committee, to persuade them to order the provincial troops under their command to repair to Newport as quickly as possible. In fact, he had just been informed by General Washington that the English intended to attack us at Rhode Island. M. de Rochambeau told me what to add on my own account, in order to supplement what he had not been able to say in the dispatch, in order to make them feel the need of this assistance.

On the 26th, at five o'clock in the morning, I mounted my horse, accompanied by a dragoon in the American service, a Saxon who had come to America with the Hessian troops in the pay of England. He spoke English, with which I was as yet unacquainted, but fortunately Latin also and very well, so that we were able to converse; it is the first time that Latin has been of use to me in this way. I explained my ideas in Latin to this dragoon, and, by translating them into English, he served as my interpreter with the people of the country. At noon, we were at Providence, a city of the same importance as Newport and more commercial; it has good anchorage and a very convenient port, suitable for trade. I got down at the house of some French merchants, to which one of their clerks whom I met on the road conducted me, and I dined with them. M. Lyon, one of these merchants, whose main house was at Boston, gave me a letter to his partner, M. Adolph, who had remained there. My horse being tired, they procured me a small carriage drawn by a horse which I drove myself. I set out at five o'clock, still accompanied by my dragoon; at eleven o'clock in the evening we were only five leagues from Boston; but we were obliged to lie at an inn. On the road and when night had arrived, as we were passing through a wood, I gave free course to my thoughts. I was 1500 leagues from my own country, accompanied by a man who had come himself a still greater distance; a strange destiny placed us beside each other for a moment.

On the 27th, I set out for Boston and arrived there at nine o'clock. I got down at M. Adolph's, who received me very well and offered me a room which I accepted. I had myself taken immediately to the

house of Mr. Bowdoin,[1] the president of the Boston
committee, to whom I handed M. de Rochambeau's
letter and another which had been entrusted to me by
M. de Corny, who was acquainted with him and had
been very intimate with him when he was in Boston.
I had a Frenchman with me, as an interpreter, called
the Chevalier de Luz, who called himself an officer.
Mr. Bowdoin caused the committee to be assembled,
agreeably to the general's letter ; and in the evening
he sent me an answer which I immediately forwarded
to M. de Rochambeau ; it was favorable and orders
had been given for the militia to repair immediately
to Rhode Island. On the 28th, I saw Mr. Bowdoin
again, in company with M. de Capellis, who had arrived. He invited us to come in the evening to take
tea at his house. We went there ; the tea was served
by his daughter, Mrs. Temple, a beautiful woman,
whose husband was a tory, that is to say opposed to
the revolution ; he had even left America and gone to
England. Mr. Bowdoin has a very handsome house ;
he is a wealthy man and respected in his country ; he
is descended from a French refugee and his name pro-
claims it. He received us politely and had a very
noble bearing. I ought not to forget that he told me
that I resembled Franklin when he was young. On

[1] Spelt Beaudoin in the original.

7

the same day we went to Mr. Hancock's, but he was
sick and we were not able to see him. This Mr. Hancock[1] is one of the authors of the revolution, as also is
the doctor with whom we breakfasted on the 29th : he
is a minister who seemed to me to be a man of intelligence, eloquent and enthusiastic.[2] He has much in-
fluence over the inhabitants of Boston who are devout
and Presbyterians, imbued, generally, with the principles
of Cromwell's partisans, from whom they are descended.
Therefore, they are more attached to independence
than any other class of people in America ; and it was
they who began the revolution.

During my stay in Boston, I dined at the house of
a young American lady, where M. de Capellis lodged.
At Newport we had seen her sister and her brother-in-
law, Mr. Carter, an Anglo-American, who had come
to supply provisions to our army. It is a great contrast
to our manners to see a young lady (she was twenty,
at the most) lodging and entertaining a young man.
I shall certainly have occasion to explain the causes
of this singularity.

The city of Boston seemed to me as large as Orleans,
not so broad, perhaps, but longer. It is, likewise, well-
built and displays an indescribable cleanliness which

---

[1] Spelt Ancouke in the original.
[2] The Rev. Dr. Cooper.

is pleasing; most of the houses are of wood ; some are
of stone and brick. The people seemed to be in easy circumstances. Nevertheless the shops were poorly stocked
with goods, and everything was very dear, which re-
sulted from the war. Their bookstores had hardly
anything but praver-books; an English and French
dictionary cost me eight louis d'or. I saw on the signs
of two shops the name of Blanchard, written like my
own, one Caleb Blanchard, the other, John.

In general, we were very well received by the Bos-
tonians, we exhibited much interest in them and made
them understand how much the king felt for them ;
we mentioned a speech of his to them, on this subject ; he said to the Count of Rochambeau who was
taking leave of him that he recommended the Americans to him, adding, " These are my real allies ; "
which, doubtless, meant that it was Louis XVI himself
who had made a treaty of alliance with them, whilst
the treaties with other allies dated from previous reigns.
Ought I to mention that M. de Volnais, the consul of
France, having taken me in his coach along with M.
de Capellis, overturned us at the corner of a sloping
street? It was a very high and open carriage, a kind
of whisky, so that we were thrown upon the pavement
and to a considerable distance. Fortunately we were
not in the least hurt, excepting the consul, who fell

upon a wound which he had received a short time before, whilst fighting a duel with another Frenchman; for he was a manslayer, my fate being to meet them everywhere. This one was a good fellow, but not very well adapted for the post which he filled.

M. de Capellis and I left Boston on the 30th and slept at Providence, which is distant 45 miles, that is to say, about fifteen leagues. The road is pleasant, we passed through some woods, where there are some pretty handsome oaks. They appeared to me to be of a different species from ours; their leaf is larger and the bark is not so smooth. We find also some pretty handsome villages, and, as it was Sunday, we continually met people who were going to the temple or returning from it, most of them in light carriages, drawn by a single horse. There are few inhabitants in this part of the country who do not own one, for, without being rich, they are in easy circumstances. They cultivate the earth themselves, with the help of some negroes; but these estates belong to them and they are owners. We also met some provincial soldiers, who, in obedience to the orders that the Boston committee had sent to them, were repairing in crowds to Newport, where, in less than three days, there would have been more than four thousand of them, if there had not been a countermand, upon the information which we received that we would not be attacked.

On the 31st, we started for Newport, where we arrived on the same day. There were ten good leagues and a ferry sometimes difficult to cross. We found that they were at work over the whole island in restoring the old redoubts made by the English and in making new ones. At this work the American militia were employed, a part of whom had been retained; our troops worked on them, for their part, so that they were in a condition to give a warm reception to the English, who had committed a great fault in not attacking us as soon as they appeared; then, whatever M. de Rochambeau said, who, nevertheless, did very well to appear secure, they might have done us much mischief; nothing was ready, few of the cannon were as yet in battery, our soldiers were sick or tired and almost all of the sailors on shore. But, in fifteen days, they had had time to recover and to make good arrangements as well for our vessels as for the land forces.

I have been very busy during the first days of August; moreover, I do not perceive any observations that appear to me to be worth mentioning, until this day, August the 13th. Since the 1st, we have remained very quiet in our island of Rhode Island. The English ships have appeared and disappeared; it has been said by turns that they would attack us and that they would not attack us; the two admirals, French and

English, have sent flags of truce to each other. Besides, we have continued to put the island in a condition of defense, with the assistance of some American troops. To-day, the 13th, there was a council of administration at M. de Rochambeau's, composed of the general officers and the commissaries. I had a very lively scene with the steward[1] respecting a purchase of meat which we have passed for the hospitals, which he had at first rejected, although he has made one subsequently for the whole army at a much higher price than that for the hospital. Our dispute arose from his having asserted that either M. Demars or I had reported that he had refused to accept an advantageous bargain, and that this was injurious to his reputation. I repeated it in every particular and answered him with a coolness and vigor of which I did not believe myself capable. The Messrs. de Vioménil, who are friendly to me, consider that I was not gentle enough towards the steward. M. de Rochambeau said nothing to me about it, but I perceived that he disapproved of my conduct. The next day I went to Papisquash with M. de Beville, quarter-master general of the army. I saw M. de Tarlé before my departure; we spoke to each other coolly, but without any explanations. On my return, I was at the

---

[1] M. de Tarlé.

quarters of M. de Rochambeau, who behaved to me as usual. But the Baron de Vioménil insisted on reconciling me with the steward; he had the kindness to take me to his house: [we embraced and all was said ;[1]] but I am afraid that this scene will be repeated, the said gentleman having ways of doing business utterly opposed to mine. He is cold, methodical, hard to please in matters of business and not very enlightened : besides he is haughty and certainly has a cold heart.[2]

On Thursday the 17th, I went to Providence with M. Demars. I have already spoken of this city which I prefer to Newport; it seems more lively, more addicted to commerce, more supplies are to be found there. We there established a very considerable hospital in a very handsome house, formerly occupied as a college.

On the 18th, after having attended to this establishment, I paid some visits in the city, first to Mr. Varnum; he had been made the commander-in-chief of

---

[1](Apparently by a later hand.) They embraced easily in those days. This fashion has passed away.

[2] All that was true, and the steward, in this instance, was certainly the first in the wrong ; but on my part, I was too warm ; I ought, either by great moderation or by some jests, to have put the laughers on my side, whereas my warmth was blamed. I have often reproached myself for this scene, and I reproach myself for it still more strongly to day (2d year of the republic). It certainly excited prejudice against me.

the militia of the country and had been styled general. I then went to Mr. Hancock's whom I have already mentioned; he has come to Providence on account of business; I was very well received by them.

On the 19th, General Varnum took me two miles from the city to a sort of garden where different persons had met and were playing nine-pins; they made us drink punch and tea. The place was pleasant and rural, and this little jaunt gave me pleasure. I was beginning to speak some English words and was able to converse. Besides, General Varnum spoke Latin. On the 20th, I dined at the house of the said general with his wife and his sister-in-law; after dinner some young ladies came who seemed well disposed to converse and to become acquainted with us. They were very handsomely dressed.

In the evening, M. Gau, commandant of artillery, who arrived from Boston, informed me that the *Alliance*, an American frigate, had just arrived. It had left Lorient on the 9th of July. The captain, named Landais, born a Frenchman, had left Lorient without waiting for the king's despatches. He wished to cruise, although laden with powder which he was ordered to bring straight to Boston; his crew, tired of his follies and his vexations, had shut him up in his cabin and had given the command of the frigate to his mate.

On board were two French officers, aides-de-camp of M. de la Fayette, and Mr. Lee, who had been a long time in France, a deputy of the congress; they told us that on the 9th of July the body of troops which they were to send to usand which they called the second division had not yet started. Besides this, they gave us no very certain news respecting the affairs of Europe.

On the 19th, I was about two miles from Providence with the health officers of the hospital to examine some waters which were said to be mineral; but we found nothing in them but a little more coolness than in the water which we use every day. This fountain is situated in a rural and pretty agreeable spot and quite near to a little wood which, by its shape, the way in which the trees were situated, their size, etc., reminded me of that which is opposite to *Les Grullieres*.[1] To-day the wind blew from the north and we were cold. This sudden change from cold to warmth causes colics; my servant Bourdais had a very violent one, a kind of cholera-morbus, which made me fear for his life.

On the 22d, I returned to Newport. I dined mid-way at Warren, in a pretty handsome inn. Not far from there there was a salt-work which I went to see. On the following days we had some councils of administration, which passed off pretty well.

---

[1] A chateau in the neighborhood of Angers (commune of Saint Sylvain), which then belonged to M. Blanchard.

I have given a list of the officers with whom I had embarked upon the Conquerant. Here now are the principal persons composing our army.

M. the Count de Rochambeau, commander-in-chief, lieutenant general.

The Baron de Vioménil,
The Count de Vioménil, } major-generals.
The Chevalier de Chastellux,

The latter discharging the functions of major-general.

De Beville, quarter-master general.

Tarlé, directing commissary, discharging the functions of steward.

Blanchard, chief commissary.

Corny, commissary. (We found him in America : he set out for France in the early part of February, 1781.)

Villemanzy, commissary.

Gau, commissary of artillery.

D'Aboville, commandant-in-chief of the artillery.

Nadal, director of the park.

Lazié, major " " "

Tucrenet.

Note from the original. De Choisy did not arrive until the 30th of September ; he had with him the Messrs. Berthier, who entered the staff. One of them was afterwards maréchal under Napoleon.

Ch⁵ D'Ogré.
Caravagne.
H. Opterre.
Turpin.

———

Coste, chief physician.
Robillard, chief surgeon.

———

Daure, steward of provisions.
Demars, steward of the hospitals.

There were also some other stewards for forage, for meat, etc; in general, too many employees, especially among the principals; all that was according to the taste of M. Veymeranges, who had arranged the composition of our army as to the administration, an intelligent man, but inclined to expense and luxury and whom it was necessary to watch.

Bouley, treasurer.

Messrs. de Menonville and the Chevalier de Tarlé, the brother of the steward, were adjutant generals.

Messrs. de Beville Jr. and Collot were quartermaster generals.

M. de Rochambeau's aides-de-camp were Messrs. de Ferry, de Damas, Charles Lameth, Closen, Dumas, Lauberdiere and de Vauban.

M. Cromot-Dubourg who arrived a short time after us, was also an aide-de-camp to this general.

The Messrs. de Vioménil also had several of them, among whom were Messrs. de Chabannes, de Pangé, d' Olonne, etc.

Those of M. de Chastellux were, Montesquieu (grandson of the president) and Lynch, an Irishman.

Colonels.

Regiment of Bourbonnois.

The Marquis de Laval.

The Viscount de Rochambeau, in 2d.

Royal Deux Ponts.

Messrs. De Deux Ponts, brothers.

Saintonge.

M. Custine.

The Viscount de Charlus (son of M. de Castries).

Soissonnois.

M. de Saint Mesme.

The Viscount de Noailles.

Lauzun's Legion.

The Duke de Lauzun.

M. de Dillon.

It is known that M. de La Fayette was not attached to our army, any more than M. Du Portail; they served with the American troops. We had in our army two officers who had served among the Americans with distinction, M. Fleury, major of Saintonge, and Mauduit, adjutant of the artillery.

On the 29th, a score of savages arrived at Newport; part of them were Iroquois. Some others came from a village called the Fall of St. Louis (situated in the environs of Albany), which is Catholic, as they asked to hear mass, on arriving. Among them was a mulatto, who had served with the Americans; he spoke French and they called him Captain Louis. There was also a German who had lived among them since he was twelve years old. The only clothing which these savages had was a blanket in which they wrapped themselves; they had no breeches. Their complexion is olive, they have their ears gashed and their faces daubed with red. There were some handsome men among them and some tall old men of respectable appearance. We also remarked two young persons at least five feet ten inches high, and one of them with a very agreeable physiognomy; some of them, nevertheless, were small. These savages, for a long time friendly to the French and who, in speaking of the king of France, called him *our father*, complimented M. de Rochambeau, who received them very kindly and gave them some presents, among other things some red blankets which had been greatly recom-

mended to us at our departure from Brest. He told
them that many of their neighbors, deceived by the
English, had made war upon the Americans, who, they
had told them, were our enemies, that, on the contrary,
they were our friends and that we came to defend them,
and that they would pursue a course of conduct agreeable to their father if they would act in the same
way and make war upon the English; he urged them
to remember this discourse well and to repeat it to
their neighbors. They dined that day with him at
his quarters. I saw them at table for an instant, they
behaved themselves well there and ate cleanly enough.
In the afternoon the troops were shown to them, who
manœuvred and went through the firing exercise;
they showed no surprise, but seemed to be pleased with
this exhibition. On the next day they dined on board
of the Duc de Bourgogne. In the evening they were
persuaded to dance; their singing is monotonous, they
interrupted it with sharp and disagreeable cries. In
singing, they beat time with two little bits of wood.
In dancing, they content themselves with bending the
hams without taking any steps; there is no jumping,
no springing; they reminded me of those peasants in
my province when they tread the grapes in the wine-
press; the movement which they then make resembles the dance of these savages. They went away on

the second of September. Some other tribes of Catholic savages had asked us for a priest; we sent them a Capuchin who was chaplain of one of the vessels.

September, 1780. We perceived after the early part of this month that the heat had considerably abated. I caused a fire to be lit on the second of September, in the evening, and I was not the only one; we began to have fogs and heavy rains. On the 6th, the Viscount de Noailles and M. de Dillon fought; the cause of the quarrel does not deserve to be mentioned.

On the 7th, I dined on board of the Conquerant, where I had not appeared since our arrival; I was very kindly received there.

On the 8th, there was a very great rain in the morning; in the afternoon the weather improved. We then had about five hundred sick, and among them a great number attacked by dysentery, this disease has been prevalent for fifteen days without appearing to be dangerous.

From the 9th, to the 11th, fine weather, and even warm. On the 11th, there was a council of administration. The tone which prevailed at it was not pleasant. I preserved profound silence at it.

On the 12th, I was at Providence with M. Corte, the chief physician; it was cloudy and we had rain. In the afternoon, we observed a plant which is very

common in the country. The botanists call it *Race-
mus Americana;* in France, it is found only in the
gardens of the botanists. We saw no other peculiar
plant anywhere else, but much wild chickory and
sorrel thorn.

I found our hospital at Providence in very good
order; we had then 340 sick there, and we had a few
more than 200 at Newport, which made the sick
amount to a tenth part of the army.

On the 13th, it was warm in the morning, but there
was rain in the evening and during the night. To-
day I walked much through the city; I especially
visited the temple which is pretty large, although
built of wood; it is very clean. I also ascended the
steeple, which, like all of them in America, is over-
loaded with carvings and ornaments, painted with
different colors ; it is likewise entirely of wood.

On the 14th, we had rain until nine in the morning; the remainder of the day was clear. I profited
by it to walk alone in the woods and upon the hills
with which the city of Providence is surrounded;
these solitary walks have always been agreeable to me.

On the 15th, rain in the morning, fine weather in
the afternoon.[1]

---

[1] I often make these remarks about the weather, the rain, the
heat and the cold, which serve to make the climate of a country

This same day, the 15th, I was invited to a party in the country to which I went. It was a sort of pic-nic given by a score of men to a company of ladies. The purpose of this party was to eat a turtle, weighing three or four hundred pounds, which an American vessel had just brought from one of our islands. This meat did not seem to me to be very palatable ; it is true that it was badly cooked. There were some quite handsome women ; before dinner they kept themselves in a different room from the men, they also placed themselves at table all on the same side, and the men, on the other. They danced after dinner to the music of some instruments of Lauzun's legion, which had been brought there expressly. Neither the men nor the women dance well ; all stretch out and lengthen their arms in a way far from agreeable. I found myself at table very near a captain of an American frigate, whom I had seen at Nantes. I perceived to-day whilst trying to converse with the ladies, that I still was very little accustomed to the English language. During dinner we drank different healths,

known. Since my return to France having seen some persons who wished to proceed to America, I have communicated these notes to them, and they have told me that they have derived more profit from them than from vague descriptions, often embellished or exaggerated.

as is usual, we to those of the Americans, and they to the health of the king of France. This extended to everybody; for on passing through an anteroom, where some negro servants were drinking, I heard them drinking together the health of the king of France.

On the 18th, M. de Rochambeau and the Chevalier de Ternay started for Hartford, in Connecticut, whither General Washington was to repair on his side for the purpose of concerting together, for it was time for them to think of making some use of our troops, who had required some indulgence on their arrival but ought not to remain useless forever.

On the 19th, we learnt that Admiral Rodney, who had been for a long time in the West Indies, had just appeared upon the coasts of America. This news surprised us and made us uneasy. We did not know whether he was followed by M. de Guichen, who had been a long while at sea. Rodney joined to Arbuthnot, ought to have about 24 vessels, most of them of three decks, and, consequently, he had a force greatly superior to ours. However, they prepared, as well on the part of the navy as of the land forces, to repel the enemy. That day we had a council of administration at the quarters of M. the Baron de Vioménil, which went off very well.

On the 20th and 21st, they continued to make arrangements for putting themselves in a state of defense. I went over the island to ascertain if there were not some pieces of ground suitable for pastures for the horses, for whom we feared that we should be in want of forage; I continued my search on the 22d, Saint Maurice's day (the patron of the Cathedral of Angers).

On the 23d our preparations for defense in case of attack were continued with success; and the longer the English delayed, the more difficult the attack became for them. It was fine weather and even very warm.

On the 24th, our military and naval generals arrived. They had had an interview with General Washington, from whom they returned enchanted: an easy and noble bearing, extensive and correct views, the art of making himself beloved, these are what all who saw him observed in him. It is his merit which has defended the liberty of America, and if she enjoys it one day, it is to him alone that she will be indebted for it.[1]

Nothing new until the 30th. This day, the frigate *La Gentille*, coming from the cape, arrived at New-

---

[1] "I wrote this in 1780. The event has shown how right I was; It is to Mr. Washington's courage, to his love for his country and to his prudence that the Americans owe their success. He has never been inconsistent, never discouraged. Amidst success as amidst reverses, he was always calm, always the same;

port; it brought M. de Choisy and some other officers appointed to our army ; they had left France on the 25th of June on a frigate which proceeded to Cape Saint Domingo, where they reëmbarked for Newport. They informed us that Monsieur de Guichen had re-turned to Europe with a considerable convoy, and that he had left Monsieur de Guichen [1] with only ten vessels.

On the same day we learnt the infamous plot and treason of Arnold, an American general. It was discovered because M. André, major-general of Clinton's army, with whom Arnold was in correspondence and who had come to the American army, was captured. Arnold, who knew it, immediately went to New York; his project was to deliver West Point, an important post upon the North river, and the loss of which would have interrupted the communication between the northern provinces and those of the south. Up to this time this Arnold had behaved like a hero, and had made a body of 6000 Englishmen lay down their arms.

October, 1780. On the 1st of October, M. de La Luzerne, the minister plenipotentiary of France to

and his personal qualities have done more to keep soldiers in the American army and to procure partisans to the cause of liberty than the decrees of the congress."—*Note from the MS.*

[1] This repetition of the name appears to be a slip of the pen.

Philadelphia, arrived at Newport to see M. de Rochambeau; he had stopped at General Washington's camp, with whom he might have been captured, if the plot which I have just mentioned had not been discovered; in the evening there was a council of administration at which M. de La Luzerne was present.

On the 2d, there was a feint of a descent; it was very fine weather, even warm, although the mornings and evenings were cold, sufficiently so to require a fire. I had not until this day some letters from France, brought for me by the frigate *La Gentille*. It is the first time in five months that I had news of my family, having started on the second of May. My brother informed me of the death of my nephew Romain,[1] a naval guard, who had gone to sea. I greatly regretted this young man, of a fine figure, and who gave promise of talents.

I also learnt that a vessel, fitted out at Brest by M. Gaudelet, laden with provisions and merchandise, which could have been disposed of to the advantage of our army, had arrived at the cape (Saint Domingo), and, for want of an escort, was unable to reach Newport; it is a pity, the merchandise would have brought three hundred per cent.

---

[1] The Count de Romain, the brother of this young man, was a fellow-student of Napoleon at La Feré.

On the 3d, I again received letters which had been left on board of the frigate and forgotten. One of them was from my wife, dated the 7th of May, written only five days after our departure. It gave me pleasure none the less.

On the 4th and 5th, cold, wind and rain.

On the 7th, another pretended attack, when the American troops played their part and manœuvred very well. Ice was seen for the first time. In the evening a kind of tempest occasioned damage to the merchantmen in port and overturned a large number of tents in camp.

On the 8th, M. de Tarlé, with whom I was living, gave a dinner to M. de La Luzerne and the generals.

Nothing remarkable on the subsequent days.

We learnt that André, that English officer, who had disguised himself to communicate with the traitor, Arnold, and who had been captured by the Americans, had been put to death, General Washington having treated him as a spy.

On the 14th, M. Holker, the consul of France at Philadelphia, a man of intelligence and great ability, arrived at Newport. A council of administration was held, in which it was resolved that I should proceed to Providence, to try to procure wood for the army, which began to be in want of it. There was none upon the island of Rhode Island, where the English, who had occupied it for some time, had destroyed all.

On the 15th, I started for Providence, as had been ordered, but having commenced my journey late, I lay at Warren and did not reach Providence until the next day. I was at Patuxet on the same day, a village a league from Providence. Then I went through a neighboring forest, where there were some portions of wood for cutting, which they proposed to us to have cut. This forest was pleasant; not very far from the place where they proposed to us to cut is a pond which reminded me of a similar site in the vicinity of Nantes. On the 17th, I returned to the forest; it was very cold, with a clear sky and sunshine. During the succeeding days I continued to be employed about my cutting, and I succeeded in making a bargain with Mr. Harris, the owner of these woods. I attended also to the means of collecting forage, which was not easy at that season. They set about it too late. Besides, the Americans are slow and do not decide promptly in matters of business. It is not easy for us to rely upon their promises. They love money and *hard* money; it is thus that they designate specie to distinguish it from paper money, which loses prodigiously. This loss varies according to circumstances and according to the provinces. Whilst I am writing, at Providence and Newport it loses sixty for one ; that is to say, a silver piaster is worth sixty paper piasters. Bills of exchange upon France, even that of the treasurer of the army upon the treasurer-general at Paris, lose 25 per cent at Philadelphia, as well as at Boston, owing to the scarcity of silver. The Americans at present owe much money in France, and they ought easily to find bills of exchange to pay it.[1] I speak of this paper money because we were beginning to make use of it in our army to pay some daily expenses, but only to the people of the country ; we should have begun with it to spare our ready money, with which, unfortunately, our chest was not well supplied.

We were unable to make use of this paper money long, because it fell completely, and no human power could have been able to raise it again.

On the 20th and 21st, alternations of cold and heat. At present, there are not more than three hundred sick, many of whom are suffering from the remains of the scurvy. I have also mentioned the dysenteries which began to prevail a month ago, but they have not proved fatal. I cannot avoid remarking that this disease, which made so much havoc in France in 1779, and especially in Brittany and Normandy, was equally

---

[1] They were not then in a condition to pay, or else they did not care about it.

fatal in this part of America in which we are dwelling; it is singular enough that an epidemical complaint should be prevalent at the same time in places so distant and separated by the sea.

On the 22d and 23d, fine weather. Three good English prizes, captured by an American privateer. The news was then circulated of the capture of Jamaica and of a considerable fleet belonging to the English and on its way to the Indies.

On the 24th, I took into the forest where I had bought wood, fifty soldiers who had been sent to me to cut it. The next day I went to see them at work; this business interested me. I love the woods. I was, in some sort, alone, far from the world. I mounted a horse and led the life of a man upon his estate.

On the 26th, I again returned to see my laborers, in the most beautiful weather. Mr. Harris, whom I met, showed me an orchard, in which he said that his father had been killed by the savages, which proves that it was not a great while ago when they were in these districts. Patuxet and Papisquash, villages and hamlets of which I have spoken, are Indian names that have been preserved.

On the 27th, in the morning, a thick fog, which dissipated at the moment of an eclipse of the sun.

At 11 o'clock it was very visible, and between noon and one o'clock it was considerable enough to darken the air. It seemed to me that it also became night some minutes after sunset. M. de Gachain, major of the squadron, took advantage of this eclipse to make some observations upon the latitude and the longitude of the coasts of Rhode Island. He sent them to the Academy of Philadelphia; he also observes that these points are exactly marked upon the map. Upon consulting an American almanac which mentioned this eclipse, I happened to cast my eyes upon the list of the princes of Europe. I read of Louis XVI, "Whom God preserve;" the same invocation upon the king of Spain; but respecting the king of England, "the sanguinary tyrant" and some words besides, the meaning of which is, born to dismember the British empire and make America independent.

I returned to Newport on the 28th; I learnt that our three frigates were gone. The *Amazone* returned to France. It had M. de Rochambeau's son on board and carried our letters.

November, 1780. On the first, rain, wind and snow. The regiment of Bourbonnois had left the camp the night before and had come to take up its quarters in the city; the other regiments came thither in succession, that is to say, they took up their winter quarters, and it appeared settled that our troops would make no movement before the spring.

From the 2d to the 6th, I remained at Providence, in cold weather; but the sun shone and I did not cease to ride on horseback and go to see my laborers in the wood. I also had much to do for Lauzun's legion, which was to proceed to Connecticut to take up its winter quarters, and which passed through Providence. All these details, elsewhere very easy, nevertheless met with many difficulties among the Americans, who dislike to lodge troops and who, as I have already mentioned, are slow and even mistrustful.

For some days past mention was made of an advantage gained over the English in Carolina, by General Smallwood; it was said that he had captured about 1500 men.

On the 9th, much snow fell and it was very cold, as was the next day. Lauzun's legion arrived at Providence to-day; it found everything that it needed. The Duke de Lauzun gave a ball, at which I was present for a moment.

On the 11th, the legion remained, the cold continued, but it was fine weather and the sun shone. I dined with M. de Lauzun.

On the 12th, the legion departed. The Chevalier de Chastellux arrived in the morning; he was on his way to General Washington's camp and thence to Philadelphia. I gave him a dinner and we paid some visits together. In conversing with him respecting the steward, whom he did not like and of whom he spoke ill to me, I remarked to him how disagreeable it was to our cloth and especially to me to have so mediocre an administrator for chief. He replied to me that when one was more than thirty, it was better for him to be the assistant of a fool than of a man of sense. He departed the next day. The ground was covered with snow.

On the 14th, a great rain. The 15th, clear and cold : it is said that the traitor Arnold has landed in Virginia with five thousand men.

On the 16th, fog and rain. M. Beaudouin, a lieutenant-colonel of Lauzun's legion, passed through Providence to go to and embark at Boston and return to France. I gave him some letters. I go regularly every day to the forest where they are busy about the wood.

On the 17th, cloudy weather, rain and very violent wind from the north-east.

On the 18th the same weather. Messrs. de Laval, de Custine and De Deux Ponts, who were going to travel in the interior of America, passed through Providence.

On the 20th and 21st, clear and cold. It is to be observed that usually after one or two days of dry cold, snow and rain follow. The same alternation in the succeeding days.

I already had much wood cut and corded; but it was necessary to transport it to the seaboard, where the vessels of the squadron had just come in search of it. For that purpose, I hired vehicles; but I had great difficulty in starting them. On the 22d I could not procure a single one on account of the rain; another time it was the cold which prevented their going. Patience and care are necessary.

On the 23d, in tolerably fine weather, I was three or four leagues from Providence, and I saw large tracts of country newly cleared and many houses recently built. This district will grow rich and become peopled gradually. I dined at Patuxet in the house of M. Dourville, a Canadian and a lieutenant in the American navy. He had married in this village where he was held in esteem; he was of great use to me for the wood-cutting which was entrusted to me. He had been employed upon the squadron of M. d'Estaing, and M. de Ternay had also employed him on his vessel.

On the 24th, it was still pretty fine and I mounted my horse according to my usual practice. I dined at Providence with Dr. Bowen, a physician and a respectable old man. He said grace before sitting down to table; he seemed beloved and respected by his numerous family and had the style and manners of a patriarch. I also dined frequently at the house of Mr. Bowker, a merchant, born in England, but for a long time settled in America. They do not eat soups and do not serve up ragouts at these dinners; but boiled and roast and much vegetables. They drink nothing but cider and Madeira wine with water. The dessert is composed of preserved quinces or pickled sorrel. The Americans eat the latter with the meat. They do not take coffee immediately after dinner, but it is served three or four hours afterwards with tea; this coffee is weak and four or five cups are not equal to one of ours; so that they take many of them. The tea, on the contrary, is very strong. This use of tea and coffee is universal in America. The people who live in the country, tilling the ground and driving their oxen, take it as well as the inhabitants of the cities. Breakfast is an important affair with them. Besides tea and coffee, they put on table roasted meats with butter, pies and ham; nevertheless they sup and in the afternoon they again take tea. Thus the Americans are almost always at the table; and as they have little to occupy them, as they go out little in winter and spend whole days along side of their fires and their wives, without reading and without doing anything, going so often to table is a relief and a preventive of *ennui*. Yet they are not great eaters.

They are very choice in cups and vases for holding tea and coffee, in glasses, decanters and other matters of this kind and in habitual use. They make use of wall-papers which serve for tapestry ; they have them very handsome. In many of the houses there are carpets also, even upon their stairs. In general, the houses are very pleasant and kept with extreme neatness, with the mechanic and the countryman as well as with the merchant and the general. Their education is very nearly the same ; so that a mechanic is often called to their assemblies, where there is no distinction, no separate order. I have already mentioned that the inhabitants of the entire country are proprietors. They till the earth and drive their oxen themselves. This way of living and this sweet equality have charms for thinking beings. These manners suit me pretty well. Burning a great quantity of wood is one of their luxuries, it is common. One-half of the districts which I have traversed are wooded, almost altogether with oaks, among which there are some very handsome ones. Yet wood is very dear owing to the difficulty of transporting it. It costs us for a league about 15 livres a cord.

I have spoken of the cups, the glasses, the paper-hangings, the carpets and other articles in which the Americans are very choice, and which they procured from England before the war. It is in this direction that French merchants ought to turn their attention by trying to bring these articles to perfection, in order to accustom the Americans to dispense with the English entirely.

On the 24th and 25th, rain and very violent west wind; the 26th to the 28th, cold and clear weather. I took advantage of it to go to Greenwich, a small town upon the coast, five leagues from Providence. Thence I proceeded to Coventry, two leagues from Greenwich. General Greene's residence is there. He is a farmer whose merit has raised him to the rank of general. He was then with the army and possessed the confidence of General Washington; he has even been commander-in-chief of a body of troops in the south; one of his brothers, an inhabitant of the country, had furnished the wagons for transporting the wood which I had caused to be cut, and he drove them himself: such are the manners of this part of America! My object was to pay a visit to the wife of General Greene, whom I happened to see at Newport and Providence. I was accompanied by M. Haake, a captain in the regiment of Royal Deux Ponts, and the chaplain

of the hospital. Mrs. Greene received us very kindly.
She is amiable, genteel and rather pretty. As there
was no bread in her house, some was hastily made;
it was of meal and water mixed together; which was
then toasted at the fire; small slices of it were served
up to us. It is not much for a Frenchman. As for
the Americans, they eat very little bread. Besides,
the dinner was long; we remained to sleep there.
Mrs. Greene's house is situated upon a barren piece of
land; this site could have been chosen only on account
of the iron-works situated in the neighborhood. There
is not a single fruit-tree, not even a cabbage. Another
country-house is pretty near, inhabited by two ladies,
who compose all the society that Mrs. Greene has; in
the evening she invited them to her house, and we
danced; I was in boots and rather tired; besides, the
English dances are complicated, so that I acquitted
myself badly. But these ladies were complaisant.

On the 29th and the 30th, I continued my trans-
portation of wood, notwithstanding the rain.

December, 1780. The month opened with a very
violent and very cold north wind.

On the 3d, snow; my friend M. de la Chèse, an
officer of artillery, had come to Providence. We
mounted on horseback together and went to dine at
Patuxet at the house of a miller's wife, whose dress,

style of living and furniture differed in no respect from the best that I had seen in the houses of the richest Americans.

On the 4th, M. de Rochambeau, who had been to Lebanon, in Connecticut, to visit the quarters of Lauzun's legion, passed through Providence; he lodged there. I gave him an account of my works which he could not visit. He departed on the 5th, in the morning. I had to make some bargains for the artillery and the navy; to the latter I had already sent some pieces suitable for building. On this head I remark that a species of oak is found in America which was very common in France and which is found there no longer, at least in the provinces with which I am acquainted; it is the white oak, mentioned by M. Buffon. This white oak was used in our old carpenter works, for which the chestnut has since been used.

From the 6th to the 12th alternations of cold, snow and rain. I do not neglect my work in the woods or in the hospital, which, being remote from the army, requires this supervision. Lastly, one hundred and twenty soldiers, of different regiments, led only by an adjutant and scattered through the woods for my labors, equally demand my whole attention.

On the 14th I went to Newport by sea in an American vessel which was struck by a gale of wind and was nearly upset; we were laden with wood, even upon deck. The cold was very severe. M. the Chevalier de Ternay, the commander-in-chief of the squadron, had been sick for several days and had just been taken on shore; M. Corte, our chief physician, had been sent for, who told us that he found him very ill.

On the 15th, M. de Ternay fell a victim to his disease; it was putrid fever. M. de Rochambeau was not then at Newport; he had gone to Boston.

On the 16th, fine weather. M. de Ternay was buried with great pomp; all the land forces were under arms.

I returned to Providence on the 17th. The same employments until the 24th; I learnt that several of our men had received letters by a vessel which had arrived at Boston from Nantes. These letters mentioned reports of a change of the minister of the navy (Monsieur de Sartine).

The 25th, Christmas-day. Fog in the morning, rain in the evening. These observations upon the weather prove that dry cold or rain does not last more than two or three days. They have not here those long spells of cold weather with which we are so often afflicted in some provinces of France. Yet I hear it said that, last year, at the same period, the sea was frozen from Newport to Providence, that is to say for a distance of ten leagues, and as broad as the Loire above Nantes. On this day we had lightning and a little thunder.

On the 27th, the sea began to freeze in the channel from Providence to Newport, and it would have done so entirely but for the violence of the wind, which agitated the water. It was Saint John's day, a great festival for the free-masons. There was a meeting of them at Providence ; it was announced in the public papers, for societies of this sort are authorized.[1] I met in the streets of Providence a company of these free-masons, going two by two, holding each other's hands, all dressed with their aprons and preceded by two men who carried long staves. He who brought up the rear and who was probably the master had two brethren alongside of him and all three wore ribbons around their necks like ecclesiastics who have the blue ribbon.

On the 28th, the Count de Vioménil and the Viscount Mesme came to lodge at Providence, and set out the next morning for Boston. Our army remaining inactive, they take advantage of it to travel and become acquainted with the country.

On the 31st I finished the cutting of my wood. My

---

[1] "*Authorized!* This note is truly French. Why authorized ? These societies, from that time were simply free in America. With us they are still only authorized."— *From the MS.*

bargain was for two thousand cords. I was very busy during these last days of the year. I paid the soldiers who had worked under me, and supplied them with the means of returning to Newport. Yet I kept some of them for another cutting of wood which I was about to undertake.

January, 1781. It was clear, the wind was from the south-west, the same weather continued on the subsequent days. At this period there was a very warm quarrel at Boston between the sailors of an American frigate, the Alliance, and those of the Surveillante, a French frigate. The Americans were the aggressors; two were killed. The two sailors who were killed were discovered to be Englishmen, in the American service, which aided in appeasing the quarrel.

On the 5th, I made two new bargains for wood.

On the 6th, Twelfth Night, [jour des Rois] the Americans had no rejoicing, no festivity.

On the 7th, melted snow and rain; on the 8th, wind from the north and sudden cold, very sharp. I saw the Chevalier de Chastellux, who was returning from his journey, with which he appeared satisfied. He told me that the Academy of Philadelphia had chosen him an associate member; that he had collected some notes respecting the American revolution, that he would not content himself with mere observations, and that he would publish a complete work.[1]

From the 10th to the 20th changeable weather. Monsieur de Rochambeau had caused a large hall to be constructed for the purpose of assembling a large number of officers therein in the evening, to afford them recreation ; they began to frequent it about this time.

On the 23d, the revolt of a body of American troops in Pennsylvania was spoken of; on the 26th, M. de Rochambeau received a letter from General Washington which informed him of the quieting of this rebellion.

On the 28th, at Providence, where I still was, I saw General Knox, who commanded the American artillery and who had acquired reputation. He was a printer and bookseller. He is a man of from thirty-five to forty years of age, of a very handsome figure ; he spent two days at Newport.

General Lincoln also came to see our troops ; he had with him Mr. Laurens, the son of a president of the

---

[1] " I do not perceive that he has kept his promise. He has had the account of his journey printed in two volumes, and some agreeable details are to be found in it, but many trifling matters, mediocre pleasantries and eulogiums, often but little deserved, of persons who had flattered him. Brissot de Warville has sharply criticised this work."— *Note from MS.*

congress, who had been captured by the English whilst on his way to Europe, and was still detained in the Tower of London. I supped, next day, with them and General Greene's wife, of whom I have spoken above.

February, 1781. M. de Corny, the commissary, was preparing to depart for France, on board of the Alliance, an American frigate which also took Mr. Laurens to Europe. I forwarded many letters to M. de Corny, especially for M. de Veymeranges and for my relation M. de Saint-James, the treasurer-general of the navy. This M. de Corny, a man of intelligence, but intriguing and greedy, was going away because there was nothing for him to do. Nevertheless, his stay in America, short as it has been, has not impaired his fortune.

On the 2d, Messrs. de Laval and de Custine returned from a long journey which they had taken in the interior of America. They confirmed the news which had been spread that the Culloden, an English ship of 94 guns, had been cast upon the coast by a violent gale of wind and had been lost. Two other English ships had been dismasted and damaged, so that, at this moment, the English squadron was reduced to six ships.

February. On the 3d, I gave a dinner to Mrs. Greene and to Mrs. Carter, and also to Messrs. de Vioménil and Chastellux. For some days past I no longer boarded with the steward, and I had procured a cook. I then kept house, at our joint expense, with M. de la Chèze, an officer of artillery, a gentleman, a deep gamester, a skillful and successful gamester, and also generous and enjoying life.

We now have snow and hail nearly every day.

On the 6th, I went to Providence and on horseback, although the roads were very slippery owing to the snow which the cold had condensed. So we met many sleighs, in which people were going on parties of pleasure or on business.

On the 7th, M. de Jumecourt, an officer of artillery, and M. Pisançon, my secretary, both very zealous free-masons, conferred on me the grade of apprentice, and in the evening I was at an American lodge where I was present at two receptions. I was then nearly 39 years old. This was beginning rather late.

From the 8th to the 13th, snow and cold; on the 13th I got into a sleigh and went twelve miles in this conveyance, which is easy and very pleasant. They go very quickly. I returned from Patuxet to Providence (five miles) in 30 minutes. I dined at the house of Mr. Flint, an American, where I learnt much news : that the Eveillé, a ship of our squadron, had just gone, with two frigates and the cutter, upon a special expedition; that an American regiment of New Jersey had imitated this revolt of the Pennsylvania troops, but that the sedition had been quickly suppressed ; two of the principal leaders had been put to death.

On the 18th, being at Newport, M. de Custine who, as I have mentioned, had just returned from traveling in the interior of America, showed me his journal and the results of his observations. This journal seemed to me to be very wise and judicious.

He agreed, as I have remarked, that the virtues of General Washington had been the strongest support of liberty. He had found the country moderately fertile, a point of view respecting which I questioned him : what I have seen of it makes me think the same; in the vicinity of our army none is found fertile except upon the banks of a river which waters Connecticut, from which we derive the greater part of our supplies of provisions.

On the 19th, we learnt that the English had been defeated by General Morgan in South Carolina. The Americans had behaved very well in this affair, in which they had charged with fixed bayonets. The account which the American general gave of this battle was very well done. The English had one thousand men, of regular troops, two hundred of whom were dragoons. The Americans had only eight hundred. We cannot conceive how regular troops and they superior in numbers allowed themselves to be beaten by peasants; they were utterly routed; the Americans took 29 officers and 500 soldiers prisoners, they captured the baggage and a large number of horses, two cannons and two flags. Although this news reaches us by an extraordinary courier, we do not receive it until a month after the event.

On the 24th, during a very strong wind, we perceived four large vessels pretty near to the shore. These vessels came in at eight o'clock. They were the Eveillé, which went out a few days before, and the two frigates; they brought with them the *Romulus*, an English ship of fifty guns, which they had captured in Chesapeake bay. They had also taken nine privateers and other small vessels, which they had burnt or left at York, a little port belonging to the Americans. But they had been unable to rejoin Arnold, on board of some vessels which had withdrawn towards the coasts of Virginia into some rivers which the Eveillé could not enter.

On the 24th, in consequence, I believe, of intelligence furnished by General Washington, orders were given to the grenadiers and chasseurs to hold themselves in readiness to start. This order was countermanded the next day, but I learnt that an expedition was in preparation, of which I was to form part, and I had to busy myself about it all the subsequent days.

We learnt on the 27th that the Astrée, a French frigate of forty guns, commanded by M. de la Perouse,[1] had just arrived at Boston after a passage of 63 days, having left Brest on the 24th of December. During the evening of the 28th, we received letters brought by this vessel. I received good news from my wife, my children and all my friends; it is not without trembling that I open their letters at this distance. M. de Montbarrey (minister of war) was succeeded by M. de Segur. Besides, there was, I was informed, an infinite amount of intrigue at the court.

---

[1] The well known navigator.

CHAPTER III.

Arrival of General Washington at Newport — Embarkation of a Body of Troops on board of the Squadron — M. Blanchard is Part of it — Naval Engagement in Chesapeake Bay — The Army commences its March to form a Junction with the Americans — M. Blanchard precedes it — He passes through Providence, Waterman-Tavern, Plainfield, Windham, Bolton, Hartford, Farmington, Baron-Tavern, Breakneck, Newtown, Peekskill-Landing — Sojourn at General Washington's Camp at Peekskill — March of the Two Armies against New York — Camps of Northcastle and Phillipsburg — Character of General de Rochambeau — The Squadron of M. de Grasse is announced — the two Armies move to support it.

March, 1781. From the 1st to the 4th, arrangements continued to be made for the proposed embarkation, which was postponed, notwithstanding.

On the 4th, a captain of the regiment of Saintonge, named Laforest, held in esteem in his corps, to whom M. de Custine had addressed some language for which he had in vain demanded justice, killed himself in despair. This event, which was known a moment before the parade, created great excitement there. M. de Custine was insulted there; and, if it had not been for the presence of some superior officers, worse would have befallen him.

On the 5th, cold and a high wind in the morning. Rain in the evening. The order was given for 1000 men of the infantry and 1500 of the artillery to embark the next day, which took place on the 6th.

This day General Washington, who was expected, arrived about two o'clock. He first went to the *Duc de Bourgogne,* where all our generals were. He then landed; all the troops were under arms; I was presented to him. His face is handsome, noble and mild. He is tall (at the least, five feet, eight inches).[1] In the evening, I was at supper with him. I mark, as a fortunate day, that in which I have been able to behold a man so truly great.

On the 7th, I repaired on board the *Duc de Bourgogne,* a ship of 80 guns, commanded by M. Destouches, who had command of this squadron. M. de Vioménil, had embarked thereon with several officers of the grenadier company of Bourbonnois; the other troops, making a total of 1120 men, were distributed among the other ships of war and the Fantasque armed *en flute ;* we also had two frigates and the Romulus, captured from the English a short time ago, and which had been brought into the line. The wind being favorable on the 8th, M. Destouches gave the signal for raising the anchor. Several vessels were already under sail,

---

[1] French feet and inches.

when the Fantasque, commanded by an auxiliary officer, made a bad manœuvre and ran aground ; fortunately after some shallops were sent to it, it was got off and was found to be free from damage ; but our departure was delayed by it for six hours, and we were unable to leave the narrow entrance to the harbor until six o'clock in the evening. The wind kept up until noon the next day : we had made 24 leagues. We steered towards Delaware bay to attack Arnold, who was ravaging Virginia.

On the 11th we were 70 leagues from Cape Henry ; the wind, favorable up to that time, became variable during the whole night, and next day we found ourselves separated from part of our vessels. We had with us only the Neptune, the Eveillé and the Surveillante. This separation was alarming ; for thus each of our divisions was very inferior to the English. We fired some volleys to find our comrades, but in vain ; unfortunately it was foggy ; at noon we had made only 14 leagues, and we found ourselves as far from the Chesapeake bay as on the preceding evening. At night, the wind became favorable, but strong. All night we had very bad weather. On the 13th, at noon, we had made 28 leagues, and were not more than 40 leagues from the bay.

On the 14th, at eight o'clock in the morning, we

saw land ; it was Cape Henry ; this shore is low, so that we were pretty near to it. We put about; soon afterwards a sail was signaled, then some others, which compels us to clear the decks for action. In the meanwhile we made signals of recognition and soon recognized the five vessels and the frigate from which we had been separated and which soon rejoined us to the great satisfaction of all. On the next day, the 15th, we tacked about to keep ourselves off the Chesapeake bay ; we were in latitude 27° 34' and in longitude 77° 53'.

On the 16th, at 6 o'clock in the morning, a sail was signaled which was perceived to be a frigate. Other vessels were soon discovered. Decks were cleared throughout our whole squadron. At 9 o'clock the English squadron was perfectly well distinguished, which formed a line after different manœuvres.

The English had eight ships, one of which was of three decks; they also had three frigates. We also had eight ships, but inferior to those of the English, for we had no ship of three decks, and we had brought the Romulus into line, which had only fifty guns. The English had also one of this force, but it was in the rank of the frigates; finally, we wanted one of our frigates, the Surveillante, detached the evening before for exploring. M. Destouches's intention was to avoid an engagement; but perceiving that the English were gaining on us considerably, he tacked about and went at them. We began the engagement at 2 o'clock; it was bad weather and there was a little rain. We were to the leeward, but that was not detrimental, owing to a heavy sea, because we were thus enabled to make use of the first battery. However, the wind changed during the engagement which lasted a little more than an hour. I will try to write an exact account of it and one prepared by a man of the service; all that I can say in the meanwhile and on my own account is, that the English seemed to me to fire very badly, that they did not take advantage of their superiority, and that there was confusion among them. One of their ships was so disabled that it fell to the leeward and made a signal of distress; it had encountered our ship and two others at the same time; if the Neptune had wished to follow it, it might have captured it or compelled it to run ashore. The Conquerant, on which I had been posted during the voyage to America, had, for its part, to sustain the attack of three of the enemy's ships, and fought hand to hand with the ship of three decks; it had also three officers killed, among others M. de Kergu, a young man of promise and of the most brilliant courage, with whom I was intimately acquainted. A hundred soldiers or sailors on board of it were hit, among whom forty were killed on the spot and an equal number mortally wounded. The greatest carnage was on the deck; the boatswains, the captain at arms and seven steersmen were among the dead, its tiller and the wheel of its helm were carried away; notwithstanding which it held out. The English, who were to the windward and, consequently, could renew the combat, were not anxious for it, put about and went away. M. Destouches's project seemed to be to follow them and attack them again; but we lost time in ascertaining the condition of the Conquerant, which had made a signal of distress.

Night came and the enemy were already at a distance. On board of the Duc de Bourgogne we had only four men killed and eight wounded; an auxiliary officer also received a contusion along side of me; the Ardent, one of the ships of our squadron, found itself for some time between us and an English ship, which warded off many blows, but at the same time was prejudicial to our manœuvre and hindered us from doing all the damage to the English that we might have done. Besides, as I have mentioned, the English did not fire well; for we were within pistol shot of one of their vessels, which twice fired a broadside at us, which I saw very plainly, without injuring us; a ball passed

13

through our mizzen-mast without rendering it unserviceable ; fourteen balls were found in the hull of the ship. During the whole of the engagement I remained upon the quarter deck, within reach of the captain and of M. de Vioménil. There I displayed coolness ; I remember that in the midst of the hottest fire, M. de Menonville having opened his snuff box, I begged a pinch of him and we exchanged a joke upon this subject. From M. de Vioménil I received a testimony of satisfaction which gave me pleasure.

On the 17th, the admiral caused us to lie to, and all the captains repaired for orders. Some infantry officers came with them, who all did justice to the valor of the naval officers and the crews. This engagement united the army and the navy. M. de la Grandiere, captain of the Conquerant, if he did not display superior intelligence, distinguished himself by his heroic courage. M. de la Clochetterie, the commander of the Jason, was also mentioned, and de Marigny, the captain of the Ardent. Lastly, M. de la Villebrune, the commander of the Romulus, of fifty guns, which sustained the shock of the London, a ship of three decks, deserved praise.

It was decided that they should return to Newport, the landing in Virginia seeming impossible in presence of the English, who, being better sailers than we, had certainly proceeded to Chesapeake bay. Besides the Conquerant was in a bad condition and the Ardent had also sustained some damage, even before the engagement. At four o'clock we set sail. The next day we did not see a single ship, and at noon we found ourselves in the latitude of 36° 6′ and in the longitude of 76°.[1]

On the 19th, they again lay by to wait for the Eveillé and the Hermione, which had chased and captured a merchantman going from Bermuda to New York. There were four English officers on board, who informed us that the English had captured Curaçao and St. Eustacia, belonging to the Dutch. M. Destouches sent the Hermione to Philadelphia with dispatches for the congress and our embassador.

---

[1] " A very exact account of the engagement was printed shortly afterwards. It will be found in the papers of the time. I am unable to find the copy which I had kept. What is certain is that the English had the worst in this affair, by which, nevertheless, we did not profit, because the Conquerant could not repair her damage quickly enough. The captain of this ship also made some mistakes in manœuvring, and lastly, M. Destouches, who was in command for the first time, and who had been unexpectedly called to this post by the death of M. de Ternay, was afraid of the court, and did not display all the energy that was requisite. The English had more cannons, but we had more men, and, I believe, more officers ; in our squadron there were some distinguished for bravery and talents."— *Note from MS.*

From the 20th to the 23d we chased two vessels unsuccessfully, one of which was a stout frigate. The winds were contrary, we tacked about and were compelled to lie by for fear of the land.

On the 23d, in the morning, there were snow, a thick fog and a violent wind from the south-east. We scattered considerably, and there was reason to fear that we might be cast upon the coast. At two o'clock the admiral resolved to spread a little sail, which diminished the danger, but exposed the Ardent and the Conquerant, already greatly damaged, to be entirely dismasted. Our hope was in a change of weather, and indeed at three o'clock the wind abated a little; at four o'clock it became more favorable, the whole crew were joyful, for they had been really uneasy, and the rather because we were unacquainted with the coast and there was a very thick fog; we had been unable to take the altitude. Besides, we were in a dangerous season and a dangerous sea. During the night the wind again became violent and the sea rough. On the 24th, the weather grew clear; three of our ships, which had separated from us, rejoined us. At last, we perceived land; it was Martha's Vineyard, eleven leagues from Newport; in the evening, we anchored near this island; but at midnight, the wind having suddenly sprung up from the north-east, we dragged our anchors and were compelled to set sail. We stood for the offing, but on the 25th at two o'clock in the afternoon, we tacked about. Our prize, from which we had been separated, rejoined us, as likewise the Surveillante, one of our frigates which M. Destouches had detached on the evening before our engagement for the purpose of reconnoitering. She reported that she had seen the English crowding into Chesapeake bay, having several ships unrigged, and that she had been hotly pursued. It was fortunate that she was able to save herself, for she was ignorant of our engagement and might have fallen into the midst of the English ships.

On the 26th, the wind being favorable, we took advantage of it to proceed to Newport, where we anchored at five o'clock in the afternoon. I landed in order to have our hospitals prepared for the reception of the wounded. I found almost all our troops still under arms, because they did not expect our return, and had mistaken us for an English squadron.

On the 27th, the troops landed; nothing of interest occurred at Newport.

The cold continued and there was ice. We had had some on board also.

April, 1781 The first days of April passed away very quietly; we received news of an engagement which had occurred on the 15th of March between the Americans and the English in Carolina. The English had remained masters of the field of battle, but with great loss of men, so that this victory had been of no great importance to them. We also had the account which the English gave of the naval engagement of the 16th of March. It was contradictory. They said that they would have gained a complete victory if three of their ships had not been greatly damaged. Three vessels disabled out of eight was not a very brilliant victory, whilst we had only two disabled.

On the 13th of April, being Good Friday, having recovered from a violent cold, I set out for Providence, where my wood-cutting had fallen behindhand, and where the hospital also required my presence : many sailors had been sent to it. I slept at Warren, it was cold and I again saw ice. As yet none of the trees had leaves, and the apple-trees, which by this time are covered with blossoms in France, had not a single one. On my arrival at Providence I resumed my old way of living which was agreeable to me, and I repaired to the wood almost every day.

On the 18th, the merchantmen, which had left Brest with us, and on which we had embarked a part of the troops and of our property, left us and repaired to Saint Domingo, under the escort of a frigate.

Nothing new to the 27th, on which I am writing. The same weather and always cold, on account of the wind which does not cease to blow strongly; these winds are one of the discomforts of this climate. Different news was then spread, as is usual among armies. I do not reproduce it, not knowing whether it is true.

On the 29th, I received the degree of master mason in a lodge held by the French, over which M. de Jausécourt presided.

May, 1781. The first days were fine and warm ; the country was still very backward.

On the 6th, I came to Newport. On the same day the Concorde, which had brought us out, arrived at Boston. The Count de Baras, chief of the squadron, appointed to take the place of M. de Ternay, and M. de Rochambeau's son [were on board]. They left Brest on the 28th of March. On the 22d of the same month M. de la Grasse had left that port at the head of a strong squadron, accompanying a considerable convoy, one part of which was for the Indies, and the other part, say 15 merchantmen, for us. These vessels were laden with goods for our army, two companies of artillery and five hundred men drawn from different regiments who were to fill up ours and be incorporated with them. I saw M. de Alpherau, lieutenant of the navy, who came with M. de Barras, and who was connected with my wife's family and knew my brother.

Since the 6th the weather has been bad enough, with alternations of rain, wind and cold; people did not begin to do without fire until about the 15th.[1]

On the 19th, eight hundred men were embarked upon the vessels which were getting ready to go to meet the convoy which we are expecting; but the English having made their appearance in superior force, it was not considered proper to send out the squadron. M. de Rochambeau set out for Hartford, on the same day, with the Chevalier de Chastellux; a meeting with General Washington had been appointed, to confer about the operations of the campaign. The bad weather returned again and we made a fire.

On the 26th, M. de Rochambeau returned from his interview with General Washington and on the suc-ceeding days made arrangements for a movement of the troops.

---

[1] " Notwithstanding this changeable weather which I have ob-served at Rhode Island during the whole winter, the country is healthy, the rest of my sojourn proved it to me. I have always had fewer sick persons in our hospitals than in France, and when our army set out in the latter part of 1782, after staying in America two and a half years, we had not ten sick in a thousand men."— *Note from MS.*

On the night of the 28th–29th, an officer of artillery named la Boroliere was assassinated by a sergeant of his company, without anyone's knowing the reason. The murderer desired to drown himself, but they drew him out of the water. The officer, although he received several blows with a sabre, does not appear to be in danger. There was no delay in the trial of the assassin, who was hung, after having his hand cut off. He did not acknowledge his crime and died with firmness.

June, 1781. The first days were fine and pretty warm. We learnt that M. de Grasse had arrived fortunately at Martinico. A council of war was held on board of the Duc de Bourgogne and decided that the squadron should not go to Boston, but should remain at Newport where we would leave four hundred men of the infantry. We continue to make preparations for the departure of the troops.

On the 4th, I spent part of the day on the island of Conanicut, with which I was not yet acquainted; it is two miles from Newport and may be about two leagues long. I was there with some naval officers and M. de la Grandiére, who had dinner provided for us.

On the 7th, the cold returned and people warmed

themselves. I was invited to a great farewell dinner
on board of the Duc de Bourgogne. There were sixty
persons present, several of whom were ladies of Newport and the vicinity. The quarter-deck had been
arranged with sails, which made a very handsome
hall. On the same day there was a council of administration, composed of officers of the land and sea services. M. de Lauzun had just arrived, after having
been to settle several points with General Washington.
In the evening M. de Tarlé told me to get ready the
next day for Providence, as the first division of the
troops was to proceed thither on the 10th.

At this period I sent some bills of exchange to
France. Our salaries were paid in money, and
we took them to the army-banker, who gave us
bills of exchange at 20, 25 and sometimes 30 premium.
I mention, for instance, that I then sent to my sister
525 livres in a bill of exchange which I had obtained
for 367 livres. It was an abuse; it seems to me that
the treasurer himself might have given us bills of
exchange with some loss to the king, but not with
that which he had to bear. There was something
odious about it; he paid us and we went as quickly
as possible to sell this money to him with usury.
At this time the American paper money was utterly

depreciated. It was at 700 per cent discount; heretofore we had seen it at from 60 to 80, and I had passed much of it at 72.

On the 9th, I went to Providence. On the road I met a naval officer, who was going to report at Newport that the Sagittaire, a ship of 50 guns, had arrived at Boston, after a passage of 80 days, with the greater part of the convoy which we were expecting. Only four ships, which had gone astray, were missing; among which was the Jauny, armed by M. Gaudelet, the correspondent of my family at Brest and my own.

On the 10th, M. de Tarlé passed through Providence on his way to Boston. The troops arrived to-day and the next day; M. de Rochambeau, the generals and the entire staff also passed through Providence. Afterwards several successes of M. de Grasse were mentioned.

From the 10th to the 16th I was occcupied with the business of the army.

On the 16th, I set out in the morning for General Washington's camp, to which I was ordered to proceed, stopping at the different places where our troops were to be stationed, in order to examine if anything was needed. The Americans supplied us with nothing; we were obliged to purchase everything and to provide ourselves with the most trifling things. It is said that it is better to make war in an enemy's country than among one's friends. If this is an axiom, it acquires still more truth when war is made in a poor and exhausted country, where the men are possessed of little information, selfish and divided in their opinions. I stopped to dine at Waterman's tavern, the principal place of the county, the first station of the army, fifteen miles from Providence, say five leagues. The road is agreeable, we pass through some woods; but we see few cultivated farms and meet with many rocks and tracts of sand. I paid nine livres for my dinner; it only consisted of a piece of veal, hastily fricasseed; but in this payment, the dinners of my two servants and of three horses were included.

At night, I lay at Plainfield, fifteen miles from Waterman's tavern. The country is a little more cleared, especially in the environs of Plainfield, where, nevertheless, there are only five or six houses I saw some farms sown with rye and wheat, but especially with maize (what we call Turkish corn in Anjou) and with potatoes. I also passed through many woods, mostly of oaks and chestnut trees. My lodging cost me 18 livres.

On the 17th, I set out at half after six for Windham, where I arrived at ten o'clock, after a journey of fifteen miles. The country is very similar to the environs of Plainfield; yet we see more pasture lands there, which are in the valleys. So we have to ascend and descend continually on this road. Plainfield and Windham are in Connecticut. Windham seemed to have sixty houses, all pretty; there is also a very handsome temple,[1] called in this country *a meeting-house.* Lauzun's legion had spent the winter at Lebanon, which is only six miles from Windham. There is another village between Plainfield and Windham, called Strickland, which seemed to me to be pretty, and where we also saw a temple. I lay at Bolton, where I was very sick, after a fatiguing march; it is eighteen miles from Windham to Boston, and we had to ascend and descend. I saw some places cleared, that is to say, where the wood had been cut, and which are tilled.

On the 18th, I arrived at Hartford, the capital of Connecticut, fourteen miles from Boston; the road is fine. Before entering Hartford we pass by a ferry across the Connecticut river, which empties into the sea and carries vessels of seventy tons to Hartford; it is not navigable any farther except for flat boats; moreover, it is not very broad. After having paid some attention to my business, I went to dine with Colonel Wadsworth, whom I had known at Newport,

---

[1] The French word for a Protestant church.

the person who supplied our army. He has a handsome house very neatly furnished. He introduced me to the governor, Mr. Trumbull, who presides over the state of Connecticut, for there is a governor in every state, chosen by the people I learnt at Hartford that General Greene, at the house of whose wife I had been at Providence, had obtained a considerable advantage in the south, and had taken 700 of the English prisoners.

On the 19th, I was particularly busy with a hospital which we were establishing at Hartford ; and I was, by way of parenthesis, compelled to fight, in presence of a great number of Americans, with three nurses who mutinied. I dined at the house of Mr. Alley, the superintendent of provisions. Hartford, the capital of Connecticut, somewhat smaller than Providence, is built in the same style ; the streets are wider, but they are not all paved. We saw there two temples, and a third outside of the city, and a Court House or City Hall. The environs are fertile, especially the banks of the river, where very good pasturage is found. Before reaching Hartford and crossing the river, we find a village called East Hartford ; it is there that our troops are to encamp. This village has only thirty houses and a temple ; but three or four miles off are some houses which depend upon it.

I did not leave Hartford until early on the 22d.   M. de Rochambeau arrived on that day with our first division, and he desired me to precede them.   I dined and remained at Farmington, ten or twelve miles from Hartford.   The country between these two points seemed to me to be dry ; but Farmington is in a pleasant valley.   I continued my journey and lay at Baron's Tavern, which is situated between two steep mountains.

On the next day, the 23d, to reach Breakneck for dinner I was obliged to follow a difficult road, to leave the valley and climb a mountain ; so that Breakneck means to break one's neck.   From this place to Newtown, where I was to pass the night, is eighteen miles, more than half of which is in a bad road.   In general, the country is middling, yet in the midst of these rocks, we find some pieces of sown ground which seem to produce much grain, at least for the time being; for these farms, newly cleared, seem to me to have little depth of soil.   At first they have produced much, because beds of the leaves of trees are found there which, being rotten and mixed with the soil, fertilize it ; but this can only be for the moment.

Newtown is on a hill surrounded by hills which are still higher.   There are only a hundred houses with two temples.   One of them was near the place where I lodged; and, as it was Sunday, I saw many people from the vicinity dismount there As all the inhabitants of the country are proprietors and, consequently, in pretty easy circumstances, they had come on horseback, as well as their wives and daughters. In the neighborhood of Boston, they come in carriages; but here the country is mountainous and the horse is more suitable. The husband mounts his horse along with his wife; sometimes there are two women or two young girls together; they are all well clothed, wearing the little black hat in the English style, and making as good an appearance as the burghers in our cities. I counted more than a hundred horses at the door of the temple, where I heard singing before the preaching, in chorus or in parts. The singing was agreeable and well performed, not by hired priests and chaplains, but by men or women, young men or young girls whom the desire of praising God had assembled.

To-day I was rejoined at Newtown, where I spent the whole day, by M. de Sançon, my secretary and some surgeons and apothecaries. I pointed out to them the site which I had selected for the hospital, and set out, on the 25th, to proceed to the American army.

I dined at Plainfield, a very small village, where I

found nothing but some fried ham and I lay at a place called Crampond. The country is mountainous and barren; the trees are small and very inferior to those in the vicinity of Providence. Crampond and its environs are not considered a very safe country; it is peopled by tories and, besides, is at no great distance from New York, where the English have their principal forces, at present.

I set out very early on the 26th and reached the American army. I stopped at Peekskill, a small village. I could hardly find a room in the inn, which was occupied by Mr. Pearson, one of the American generals. Peekskill is situated on the North river which is very broad; it is almost an arm of the sea, which vessels of war ascend. In some respects it divides America into two parts, and it is upon this river that the fortifications of West Point are found, the important post which Arnold had intended to give up to the English. I went to speak to General Pearson, who gave me an aide-de-camp, to conduct me to General Washington, whose quarters were at a distance of two miles. I found him sitting upon a bench at the door of the house where he lodged. I explained my mission to him and he gave me a letter for the quarter-master of Peekskill landing, to which I proceeded. These quarter masters have here, in the

15

army, almost the same functions as we, but with more authority. I set out immediately upon the same horses, although I had more than eight leagues to travel and in the rain. I passed through another Peekskill where the Americans have their magazines and their arsenals. These are large wooden barracks, built recently, situated between two ranges of mountains. This other Peekskill is on the bank of the river; it is there that they are building our ovens, a business which I found very little advanced. The builder, desiring to make them elegant, sent to a distance for the materials. The next day I went to Poughkeepsie, a village where it was proposed to establish our hospitals, five leagues beyond Peekskill landing, on the road to Albany, and, consequently, to Canada. I sent a letter to General Clinton, which I had for him; he is the governor of the province of New York, in which we were. The legislature was then sitting, to which I was summoned, the governor having informed them of my demand of a site to establish a hospital. After waiting for some time, two deputies were sent to me who spoke French, General Schuyler, retired from the service and residing at Albany (he was brother-in-law of M. Coster, one of the providers of our army); the other, General Scott, commanding the militia of the province, both about

50 years of age and of good manners. On tne same day I returned to sleep at Peekskill landing. It is a village partly inhabited by Dutch families. They have preserved the manners and character of their nation. The inn at which I dismounted was kept by one of these families.

I set out again on the 28th for the American army. I passed by General Washington's quarters, but as he had changed them I did not see him, and I proceeded directly to the inn at which I had previously dismounted at Peekskill. I met M. Du Portail, a French engineer in the service of America, with whom I conversed. He was greatly esteemed by the Americans. I spent the remainder of the day in the camp and saw two regiments go through their exercise. The soldiers marched pretty well, but they handled their arms badly. There were some fine-looking men; also many who were small and thin, and even some children twelve or thirteen years old. They have no uniforms and in general are badly clad.

On the 29th, I got on horseback to see some barracks which had been occupied by an American regiment during the winter; my purpose was to establish a hospital there. On the road I met General Washington, who was going to review a part of his troops. He recognized me, stopped and invited me to dine with him at three o'clock. I repaired thither; there were twenty-five covers used by some officers of the army and a lady to whom the house belonged in which the general lodged. We dined under the tent. I was placed alongside of the general. One of his aides-de-camp did the honors.

The table was served in the American style and pretty abundantly : vegetables, roast beef, lamb, chickens, salad dressed with nothing but vinegar, green peas, puddings and some pie, a kind of tart, greatly in use in England and among the Americans, all this being put upon the table at the same time. They gave us on the same plate beef, green peas, lamb, &c. At the end of the dinner the cloth was removed and some Madeira wine was brought, which was passed around, whilst drinking different healths, to the king of France, the French army, etc. I rose when I heard General Washington ask for his horses, because I desired to have a conversation with him and Mr. Coster, the purveyor of our army, who had arrived and spoke French well. We all three left the table; the other officers remained ; the lady also withdrew at the same time as we. Our conference being ended, the general proposed to us to return again to the table for a moment, whilst waiting for the time of departure. Again some healths were drunk, among others that of the Count de Grasse; then everyone rose from table. I have dwelt upon the details of this dinner, because everything that relates to General Washington seems interesting to me.

I have already described his figure. His physiognomy has something grave and serious; but it is never stern, and, on the contrary, becomes softened by the most gracious and amiable smile. He is affable and converses with his officers familiarly and gaily. I was not sufficiently accustomed to the English language to maintain a connected conversation with him; nevertheless we exchanged some words, for instance, respecting the battle of the Chesapeake, which he considered glorious to our arms. He excused himself respecting the entertainment which he had given me, to which I replied that I found myself in good case in America, better than in Corsica, where I had been for a long time. As to this subject he told me that the English papers announced that the Corsicans were about to revolt and create a diversion against us. I replied that I had no fear of it, that the Corsicans were not dangerous, and that Paoli was not Washington. In the evening I saw him again; he had come to see General Pearson, in whose house I was lodging. He invited me to come and dine with him as long as I remained in his quarters. On the next day, passing by this house, again, he stopped there, caused me to be called, and proposed to me to take me to dine at the house of one of the American generals to which he was going. I thanked him, on account of some business, and he invited me in the most polite manner in the world for the next day.

July, 1781. I went thither, indeed ; it was the first of July. I found the table served as at the first time with about the same number of guests. I was alongside of General Washington and another general named Lord Stirling (he claimed to be an English lord). General Washington seemed, for a moment, to be somewhat absent, at other times he joined in the conversation and appeared to be interested in it. There was a clergyman at this dinner who blessed the food and said grace after they had done eating and had brought on the wine. I was told that General Washington said grace when there was no clergyman at table, as fathers of a family do in America. The first time that I dined with him there was no clergyman and I did not perceive that he made this prayer; yet I remember that, on taking his place at table, he made a gesture and said a word which I took for a piece of politeness, and which perhaps was a religious action. In this case, his prayer must have been short; the clergyman made use of more forms.

We remained a pretty long time at table. They drank twelve or fifteen healths with Madeira wine. In the course of the meal beer was served and *grum,* rum mixed with water.

On the 2d the American army left the camp of Peekskill to advance nearer to New York. The first division of our troops proceeded in the same direction. I was informed of this march, the evening before, by M. de Tarlé, which altered our projects of establishments for victuals and hospitals in the environs of Peekskill, where I was, nevertheless, obliged to remain. General Washington himself departed, and I saw him pass with his staff and an escort of dragoons.

On the 3d, I learnt that our army was at Northcastle. I ought to send bread to it. Only a small quantity, 3000 rations, reached me. The ovens of Peekskill landing were found to be too distant from our army, and this service was not well performed. Besides, I was not entrusted with it and had very little authority over it.

On the 4th, in the morning, I saw several American officers returning wounded to Peekskill; they had been so the evening before at Kingsbridge. The English were guarding a post there which the American advanced-guard attacked; one of these officers was stretched out in the room in which I was dining;

his wife was busy about him and dressed his wounds
herself, a touching spectacle, but little suitable for
giving an appetite. On the same day, the effects of
the American troops which had remained at Peekskill were sent to them upon a great number of vehicles,
escorted by some soldiers of this nation, who, contrary
to all discipline, fired incessantly and thus spent their
powder very uselessly, a commodity which, nevertheless, was very scarce in America.

On the 5th, I rejoined the army at Northcastle. It
left that place on the 6th. I remained at Northcastle
to establish a hospital there. On the 7th, I rejoined
our troops, encamped at Phillipsburg, eight leagues
from New York. I lay in M. de la Chèze's tent, not
having my baggage with me. The heat was excessive;
it was not moderated until the 10th by a great rain
which lasted all night and passed through all the
tents. I dined that day at the intendant's with
General Washington. He was rather grave; it was
said that there had been a little misunderstanding
between him and General Rochambeau. General
Washington's army was encamped near ours; it was
about 4000 men.

On the 11th, I returned to Northcastle to see our
hospital establishment; I busied myself until the 14th
in the details of the service. I learnt some particulars

respecting the attack of Kingsbridge, of which I have spoken; they expected to surprise the English, but they were upon their guard, so that the Americans were repulsed. Lauzun's legion marched to their assistance; but General Lincoln, who was retreating, did not think fit to employ it. We had news that the English were evacuating Virginia, which, it was said, was to be ascribed to the march of our troops. Lastly an engagement was mentioned between the Surveillante, a frigate of our squadron and a ship of 50 guns; she got off with much glory; she was commanded by M. de Villars. It is the same frigate that fought with so much courage against another English frigate which took fire; she was then commanded by M. de Conedie, who received a wound of which he died.

On the 15th, I returned to the camp. In the evening M. de Rochambeau reproached me respecting the supply of bread which had failed. It was in vain for me to justify myself by telling him that I was not especially entrusted with this service; he was unwilling to listen to me. Nevertheless I had foretold that the bread would fail owing to the remoteness of the ovens. Next day the following remarks of M. de Rochambeau were related to me, that I was well pleased to see the supply fail, because I wished to have the intendant sent away and to fill his place;

that as to the rest, the provisions ought to have been entrusted to me. Never were reproach and suspicion more unjust, and I felt it much. But such is M. de Rochambeau. He mistrusts every one and always believes that he sees himself surrounded by rogues and idiots. This character, combined with manners far from courteous, makes him disagreeable to everybody.[1]

On the 17th, I had occasion to see him again and he charged me to go and reconnoitre a site where he proposed to esbablish new storehouses of provisions, which I performed the same day. On the next day I wasted a whole day in running over, tediously and uselessly, the environs of the camp in a barren and desert region with which I was unacquainted, to find some employees whom I needed. Nevertheless, I succeeded in having

---

[1] I wrote what precedes in a moment of ill-humor; and although M. de Rochambeau was unjust to me, on this occasion, and there is some truth in the portrait, which is here drawn of him, I ought to say that he also has good qualities, that he is wise, that he desires what is good, and that, if he is not an able administrator, he is generally very active, having an excellent glance, readily becoming acquainted with a country, and understanding war perfectly. He has served well in America and has given a favorable idea of the nation. People expected to see a French fop, and they saw a thoughtful man. "Your general is abstemious," an American alongside of whom I was dining, once said to me, and who remarked his moderation at table. This moderation and this wisdom were generally observable in the most important points.

a service of provisions established in a village called Rick's mill. On returning to camp I learnt that a captain of Lauzun's legion had been killed whilst going the rounds with the patrol.

On the 21st, I saw M. de Rochambeau, to whom I gave an account of what I had done. His reception of me is usually cold. Nevertheless, I knew that he had spoken of my performances with praise. In the evening, at 9 o'clock, Lauzun's legion and the grenadiers and chasseurs of the Bourbonnois brigade started under the command of M. de Chastellux for an expedition, of the cause and object of which we are ignorant. An American corps also marched. M. de Rochambeau and Washington followed these divisions.

We learnt, on the 22d, that these troops had not accomplished anything, and they returned on this same day after having pillaged extensively and committed disorders, of which hitherto there had been no example. On the contrary, the army had behaved with a prudence which had merited the greatest praises from the Americans themselves. The latter marched in a very orderly manner to-day. I believe that they had no other object than to make a reconnoissance, the result of which was to satisfy them that they could not attack New York without very superior forces.

Nothing new happened until the 26th, when I re-turned to Northcastle. At this time it was said that the English fleet had left New York, to go to Virginia in search of Lord Cornwallis, who seemed to be desir-ous of evacuating that province altogether. If this news is true, the English must be very strong in New York, which ought to oblige us to retreat and to evacuate the camp of Phillipsburg : that would not be much re-gretted as to the matter of convenience. The head-quarters especially are badly situated and all the corps and services too distant from each other. I was obliged to go four or five leagues every day to attend to my business.

The country is uneven, cut up by hills and woods. It is hard to find any valleys at all fertile. The hos-pital, for instance, was located on a farm, the truly rural situation of which was very pleasing. In these fields we saw two trees which are met with in France only in the gardens of the botanists and of some con-noisseurs ; the tulip tree and the catalpa. The first is of the poplar genus ; it becomes very tall and very straight ; its bark is handsome and its leaf large ; it has a flower which resembles a tulip, whence its name. I saw one at Northcastle taller than the finest elm and as thick, straight and affording much shade ; this would be a fine tree for an avenue ; the other the catalpa, or the caltapa, resembles the plantain, but its leaf is larger; the flower resembles that of the horse-chestnut; it bears it at the same time as the leaves. This would be a very suitable tree for ornamenting gardens and making arbors. It is known in France by the name of bignonia, a name which Tournefort had given it in honor of the Abbé Bignore, the keeper of the king's library. In conversing with the Americans about agriculture, I became confirmed in the opinion that the farms which appeared fertile in the north of America were chiefly so because they were newly cleared, but that they soon become exhausted. It is said that better soils are found on penetrating to the west. I am willing to believe it, but this country is unknown and inhabited by savage tribes, difficult to be subjugated.

August, 1781. Nothing interesting occurred during the first days of the month. I went and came, from the camp to Northcastle and from Northcastle to the camp. Pretty often we had storms and heavy rains, which cooled the air only for a moment. We had few sick men and less in proportion than in France. The retirement of M. Necker was much spoken of at this time, which seemed to concern everyone. We learnt this news through the English, who often sent trumpets and forwarded gazettes to us. We learnt from the same papers that M. de la Mothe-Piquet had captured a rich convoy. The parleys between us and the English were displeasing to the Americans, and even to General Washington; they were unaccustomed to this way of making war.

We were very quiet in our camp, foraging without being disturbed. The English contented themselves with guarding their cities and the outposts without making the least attempt against us; this made us sometimes believe in peace. On the other hand we were in daily expectation of M. de Grasse's squadron.

On the 16th, having gone to Peekskill to see our magazines and two churches which I was fitting up to serve as hospitals for us in case of need, I received an express from the intendant telling me to transfer the hospital from Northcastle to Peekskill; he added that he was about to proceed to Chatain on the North river. I proceeded immediately to the army, taking another route than the usual one. I skirted the North river and passed through a village called Taristown,[1] where there was a little trade. On arriving at headquarters, I learnt that the Concorde frigate, detached by M. de Grasse, had just arrived and that it had brought dispatches from him. He announced that he was about to join us with twenty-eight ships of the line; as, ac-

---

[1] Qu. Tarrytown?

cording to all appearances, he must have entered Chesapeake bay, the French and American generals made a movement with the two armies to be nearer to him and to confine, or rather to hem in, Cornwallis's army which was at the extremity of Virginia. This frigate confirmed to us the capture of a convoy by M. de la Mothe-Piquet; we also learnt that they had recaptured Pondichéry and were besieging Madras. It seemed also that the news of the retirement of M. Necker was assuming consistence.

On the 19th, the army began its movement to the rear from Phillipsburg to Northcastle. Many wagons broke down on the road and there was much disorder in the columns; a very great rain which came on delayed the march, and the troops bivouacked on the road. M. de Rochambeau had a very lively scene with the intendant upon this subject; I was present and suffered much on account of it. I thought that if these positions are handsome they certainly have their discomforts.

On the 21st, the army left Northcastle. In the evening I received orders from the general to carry a letter to General Washington, who was already on the other side of the North river, where we also were beginning to form some establishments. The Americans were already much farther off than I had supposed; I joined them, nevertheless : General Washington was occupying Smith's house, famous owing to the fact that there André and Arnold had held their meeting. General Washington was taking tea ; I took it with him. He read the letter, which I had brought him, twice, and which, I believe, contained nothing very important. When he had given me his answer, I immediately set out again ; it was late and I crossed the North river by night ; I reached head quarters at eleven o'clock. All the rooms were occupied in the inn where I alighted, and I slept on the floor and upon a staircase.

The next morning I learnt that some letters had arrived for us by the frigate la Magicienne, which had just reached Boston after a passage of fifty-three days, and which brought us 1,800,000 livres. Another frigate, la Fortune, which had put into St. Domingo, followed her closely. The retirement of M. Necker is confirmed. M. de Vioménil received a memoir composed against him, which he communicated to me, and which seemed to me a little masterpiece of wit.

CHAPTER IV.

The Allied Armies cross the North River and march towards the Chesapeake Bay — M. Blanchard rejoins them soon afterwards — He passes through Whippany; Somersèt, Princeton and Redlines, stops at Philadelphia, and goes on through Chester, Wilmington, Brandywine, Christian Bridge and Head of Elk, where he rejoins the Army — He embarks with a Detachment to effect a Junction with the Troops brought by M. de Grasse's Squadron, which had arrived in the Bay.

August, 1781. On the 22d and 23d, the army began to cross the North river, and it was decided that I should remain for the present at Peekskill.

On the 23d and 24th, our troops finished crossing the river. This crossing occupied much time, owing to the breadth of the river, which they were obliged to cross in ferry boats collected in great numbers, but still not enough. On the 25th, I went myself to the spot and saw many of the troops and much baggage cross. General Washington was there; they had provided a pavilion for him, from which he examined everything very attentively. He seemed, in this crossing, in the march of our troops towards the Chesapeake bay and in our reunion with M. de Grasse, to see a

17

better destiny arise, when at this period of the war, exhausted, destitute of resources, he needed a great success which might revive courage and hope. He pressed my hand with much affection when he left us and crossed the river himself. It was about two o'clock. He then rejoined his army, which had commenced its march in the morning, as also the first division of our army.

On the 26th, the second division of our army and all our troops directed their course towards Philadelphia. The American general Heath was entrusted with the command of this side of the river and the protection of our establishment.

On the 28th, after having caused a convoy for the army to set out, I mounted a horse to go to West Point. It is a fortification, or rather a mass of fortifications, erected upon a rock which projects much into the river and contracts it considerably at this place. The passage of it was difficult and the Americans had neglected nothing to increase the natural difficulties. Thus the English had never dared to attempt this important crossing. West Point is the post which the traitor Arnold wished to give up in the latter part of

---

Note. The event has justified my remarks ; for the capture of Yorktown, the result of our reunion with M. de Grasse, greatly contributed to the peace and secured the liberty of America.

1780. The Americans have some establishments in the neighborhood, among others, a hospital which I visited; the sick were in single beds, but without sheets and only on the straw with a coverlid. Besides, they had no nourishment but bread and meat which the convalescents prepare. The buildings which serve for the hospital were nothing but barns which had not even been repaired.[1] People sometimes complain of our military hospitals, but it is enough to see these to acknowledge that these complaints are unfounded. Military men who have traveled know it well and declare that our army-hospitals are greatly superior to all those of foreign countries. From West Point I went to Peekskill, where I had already been in the month of June. As I was passing in the midst of some barracks connected with the American establishments, I was greatly surprised at hearing French spoken. In fact, these barracks were occupied by eight or ten families who had come from Canada; the men had been employed among the troops and the women and children had been left in these barracks, and some assistance had been given to them. They

---

[1] Let the reader consult the work of the sub-intendant Vigo-Roussilon, *Of the Military Power of the United States of America*, 186, and let him compare the American hospitals of 1781 with those of the War of the Succession.

presented a very miserable appearance. A woman to whom I spoke, twenty years old and of a tolerably pretty figure, called herself by her maiden name, Marie Goguet. She spoke pretty good French without accent. I gave her a piaster, which she received with pleasure. On the 30th, I crossed the North river at King's-ferry, and, having concluded to rejoin the army, after having given my instructions, I set out on the first of September.

September, 1781. The country which I crossed for three or four leagues is mountainous and middling, it is better and more agreeable in the place where I stopped to dine, at Suffern, which is also the name of the inn-keeper. His house is situated in the state of New York; but Pompton, where I passed the night, is in New Jersey. The road to it is very level, it is in a valley tolerably well cultivated and pleasant. I lodged at the house of a Dutchman, John Van Gelder, who received me very well. The next day, at two, I dined at Whippany, where the army had stopped. The road which I followed continues to be fine, situated in a cultivated valley. Some wood is found there nevertheless. I observed fewer apple trees there than in the other provinces through which I had passed, but many peach trees. This valley is also very narrow and the mountains which border on it are barren;

there are some sandy places in the valley itself. I
saw nothing there but buckwheat and maize, and
these farms are greatly in need of manure. In France
these farms would be middling good. I learnt, on the
way, that the *La Resolute* frigate had arrived ; we
were impatiently expecting it ; it had been announced
to us by the Magicienne. It brought us money, as
well for us as for the Americans, and some goods for
their troops. It also brought back Mr. Laurens, the
son of a president of the congress, whom I have already mentioned, and who had gone to France in the
month of February to ask for this assistance. On the
same day I came to spend the night at Bullion's tavern, after having passed through Chatham, a village
where our ovens had been set up, which I was well
pleased to visit, which caused me to go five miles farther and prevented my passing through Morristown,
where General Washington had his quarters for a
long time, and where the Americans have some iron-
works as at Peekskill ; I also lost the opportunity of
visiting the country house of Lord Stirling, that
American general whose nobility is somewhat con-
tested. This country house is almost unique in these
parts, where the dwellings resemble farm houses ;
they have no gardens, no fences, no fruit-walls, only
some apple trees, some peach trees and some scattered

cherry trees, or forming what we call orchards. The road which I took to reach Bullion's tavern is not disagreeable ; but the farms are still middling, they were sown with maize and buckwheat; I also saw a little hemp there.

On the 3d, I dined at Somerset, the same kind of country and the same road, and lay at Princeton, a pretty village, of about sixty houses ; the inns there are handsome and very clean. A very handsome college is also to be seen there, built in the same style as that at Providence. The English had quartered their troops in it when they were masters of this part of the country ; they had damaged it somewhat. I visited the college ; there were fifty scholars ; there was room for two hundred. Several languages were taught ; a student who accompanied me already spoke a little French.

He showed me a tolerably ingenious machine representing the movement of the stars, which was moved by springs. My intention had been to spend the night at Princeton, but the weather was fine and I proceeded to Trenton, going forty miles in the day. Trenton, ten leagues from Philadelphia, is a pretty considerable village, of at least a hundred houses, situated on the Delaware. This village, or little city, is pretty and seems to announce the vicinity of a capital. I made haste to leave it on the 4th, having learnt that our first division was already at Philadelphia, and that the second arrived there on this very day. I crossed the Delaware in a ferry boat; it is neither broad nor deep at this place, but at the distance of four leagues it becomes as broad as the Loire below La Fosse. I had heard Americans say that these two rivers resembled each other; this resemblance also struck me owing to the colors of the white and limpid water and the low and agreeable banks. The road leading to Philadelphia is fine, at least to within ten miles from this city, at Redlines,[1] where I stopped to dine and wrote these notes. It is quite wide and skirts the Delaware; forests are passed through in some places. At last, I reached Philadelphia in the evening; the country in the neighborhood is cultivated; here and there I met with pretty houses and everything announced the vicinity of a great city. Philadelphia is a very extensive city, and regularly built; the houses are of brick and pretty high, the streets straight, broad, and very long; there are side walks for persons on foot. Some public buildings are also to be seen there which are worthy of a great city, such as the house where the congress meets, the hos-

---

[1] The Red Lion?

pitals and the prison. The absence of quays upon the
Delaware deprives it of a great convenience and a
great beauty. In the evening I repaired to the house
of M. de la Luzerne, who was giving a great dinner to
the chief officer of the congress, General Washington
and the principal officers of our troops. On entering
the city they defiled before the president of the congress and saluted him. Beginning on the 5th, our first
division set out for the Chesapeake bay. I walked
much in the city, without neglecting my business and
the attention to be paid to our sick, who had been
quartered in the Philadelphia hospital. I dined on the
same day at the house of M. de la Luzerne with more
than eighty persons. Whilst we were at table, news
was brought that M. de Grasse had arrived in Chesapeake bay with twenty-eight ships of the line, and
that he had landed three thousand men who had joined
M. de la Fayette, so that Cornwallis, who found himself between the fleet and the land forces, was in danger of being captured. This news was received with
great joy by all the guests, French and Americans.
In the evening the citizens assembled and proceeded
in a crowd to the hotel of the ambassador. During
the day, the regiment of Soissonnois had manœuvred
before a crowd of the inhabitants, who seemed to ad-
mire the fine appearance of the soldiery and their

discipline. The tories could not avoid agreeing to it, but they said that it was a regiment recruited in England. The English had described us to the Americans as pigmies.

On the 6th, the second division commenced its march. M. Holker, the French consul at Philadelphia, took me to dine at his country house, only three miles from the city. We drank some excellent Burgundy wine, which is very scarce beyond the sea. Several French merchants were at this dinner.

On the 7th, after having breakfasted at the house of our ambassador, I set out to rejoin the army, and lay at Chester, after having crossed the Schuylkill one mile from Philadelphia, at the place where M. Tronçon-Du-Coudray, a well-known officer of artillery, who had been sent to the Americans, was drowned in crossing a ferry. At present there is a bridge. Chester is a little village, five leagues from Philadelphia and on the Delaware. The next day I started early and lay at Wilmington, a village upon the Brandywine, whereon an important battle was fought which has retained its name. Thence, I went to dine at Christian Bridge, where I did the honors of the public table to some Americans with whom I drank toasts. At night, I lay at the Head of Elk, where I found our army. The country through which I had passed for two days

18

was, generally, barren and sandy, so that we were covered with dust.

On arriving, I learnt that 1200 of the troops, of whom a part were grenadiers and chasseurs, were to embark for the purpose of joining the troops which M. de Grasse had brought, and that I was to be on this expedition. They were to embark on a little river leading into Chesapeake bay; the remainder of the troops were to proceed by land to the appointed spot; that is to say in front of York to which Cornwallis had withdrawn.

On the 9th, I devoted myself to the embarkation. On the 10th the boats provided to convey us repaired to Plumb Point, where the embarkation was easier, and on the 11th they were on board. In company with M. de Custine I got on board a small boat, in which were smoe officers and fifty grenadiers. Cooking could not be done on these boats and we had nothing but some biscuits and cheese for the soldiers, and some cold meats for us. On the 12th, in the morning, we had not made much headway, the wind being contrary, yet we entered Chesapeake bay on the same morning. At this point it is a league in breadth. This Chesapeake bay is a little Mediterranean, and some immense rivers empty into it which bear the largest ships, such as the Potomac. On the evening of the said day, the

12th, a storm of wind and rain came on, so that we were compelled to anchor. We were cruelly tossed about all night and almost everyone was sick. We were then as high up as Annapolis and in sight of two frigates and a cutter which the bad weather did not allow us to join, and which we supposed to form a part of M. de Grasse's squadron. Next day we had fine weather and continued to advance; but we were not followed by the other boats, twenty in number. We perceived a pretty strong boat coming towards us by the use of oars; we did not pay much attention to it, when suddenly it tacked about and left us. We suspected that it was a little pirate (there are many of them in these parts); desiring to attack us it concluded on approaching that we had too many people on board.

On the 14th, we joined M. de Grasse's squadron and M. de Custine, and I went on board of the *Ville de Paris* which he commanded. He received us very well and gave us dinner. We learnt that he had had an engagement with the English squadron a few days before. M. de Grasse had the advantage, but he did not pursue the English because he was unwilling to leave the Chesapeake bay, the rather because he was expecting the ships which M. de Barras was bringing to him, and which we had left at Newport when the army departed from that city in the month of June.

They might have been intercepted by the English, but fortunately they joined M. de Grasse.

Two days afterwards, the squadron having left the bay, two English frigates entered it to cut loose the buoys of the squadron which had been left there; they had not time to escape, and were captured upon the return of the squadron.

M. de Grasse's squadron, after its junction with M. de Barras, was composed of more than forty ships or frigates. I saw several naval officers of my acquaintance, and was on board of the Duc de Bourgogne. Then being in haste to land, I hired a little American boat on which I embarked with M. de Lauberdiere,[1] who had followed M. de Custine. We were to ascend the James river and join M. de la Fayette, to inform him of our arrival, and that I might prepare everything that was necessary for the arrival of our troops. There was some imprudence in embarking in so small a boat and upon a very stormy river, and I heard it mentioned to M. de Grasse who saw us start from his stern-gallery. We had scarcely room to lie down in this little boat, and we were in the open air. It rained the next day, and we were penetrated to the skin. Moreover the captain was very little acquainted with

---

[1] An aide-de-camp to M. Rochambeau.

this river, and there were many sandbanks so that we touched several times.   At last, after having wandered for a long time in an unknown river, we landed two leagues from Williamsburg, where M. de la Fayette was posted; at least that is what a woman told us whom we met.   There was no house or place where we landed, and we were compelled to go a long way on foot.   At length we arrived at a deserted house where were two persons who let us in, but neither furniture nor provisions.   We lay upon the floor. The next day, having hired horses, we proceeded to Williamsburg, the capital of Virginia.   It consists of only a single street, but very broad and very handsome.   Two or three public buildings, pretty large, are also to be seen there.   We got in at the quarters of M. de la Fayette, where I found M. de Chastellux, who had arrived the evening before, with M. de Rochambeau and M. de Washington.   They had got in advance by making forced marches across Maryland and Virginia.   This latter province is General Washington's birthplace; he has there a very handsome dwelling-house, where he received our two generals : he had not been in his own country since the beginning of the war.   A body of Americans under the command of M. de la Fayette were encamped near Williamsburg.   Three French regiments, which M.

de Grasse had brought, were joined to them, forming a body of 3000 men. They were the regiments of Gatinois, d' Agenois and Touraine. I found among my acquaintances the Count d' Autichamp, who commanded one of the regiments ; he spoke much to me of my uncle, settled in St. Domingo, with whom he was connected. From this day, I set to work, although without a piece of paper or an employee or a bag of flour at my disposal : I was completely overwhelmed, which I still remember now that I am copying this thirteen years afterwards. The Baron de Steuben, a German general officer in the service of America, gave a great dinner to our generals, and I went to it. The next day the French and American generals, went on board of the *Ville de Paris* to see M. de Grasse. I sent a note to M. de Rochambeau to obtain some supplies from the navy in wines, flour, &c. On the 17th and the following days I worked much with M. de la Fayette, who was pleased to assist me in providing for our troops. It is difficult to employ more order, patience and integrity in the discussion of business matters ; he reminded me of Scipio Africanus in Spain ; as young and as modest as he, he already had the reputation of a skilful warrior ; for the last campaign which he had just made, whilst sustaining himself against Cornwallis with inferior forces, had procured him much glory, and justly so.

On the 21st and 22d my work was doubled ; I caused ovens to be constructed, but I was in want of tools and I had to run about much and negotiate to obtain even a hammer. Our generals came and deposited with me 800,000 livres in piasters, which M. de Grasse had brought for us. The grenadiers and chasseurs also arrived ; everybody applied to me for bread, vehicles and all possible necessaries. I was alone and had not a single employee to assist me. On the 23d I was sick, owing to fatigue ; I had spent part of the previous nights on my feet. In the evening I threw myself on a bed ; fortunately two employees arrived who made a report to me and to whom I gave orders from my bed. During the night, as I was more oppressed than drowsy, the floor of the chamber adjoining that in which I was suddenly broke in pieces with a great noise. This accident proceeded from the money which I had deposited there ; it was on the ground floor and underneath was a cellar, fortunately not very deep : the floor, being too weak, had been unable to bear the weight of these 800,000 livres in silver. My servant, who lay in this room, fell down the length of a beam, but was not hurt.

At last, on the 25th, the intendant arrived, as well as M. de Villemanzy, the commissary of war. In the evening we had a conference with M. de Rochambeau ;

we were then in the greatest anxiety on the subject of subsistence. The country in which we were was exhausted by the Americans and laid waste by the English; and our troops which had made forced marches could not be followed by the magazines. A vessel forming a part of M. de Barras's squadron was anchored near to us, laden with flour which it had been to procure at Baltimore or Annapolis, for the squadron. I persuaded M. de Rochambeau to ask M. de Villebrun, who commanded this vessel, and with whom we were all well acquainted, to spare us a part of this flour; I undertook to draw up the letter and it had the desired success. I note it because M. de Rochambeau, often fearing to compromise himself, had on this occasion a sort of repugnance to writing, and this feeling was often injurious to him.

On the 27th, M. de Chastellux had a very lively and very unbecoming scene with M. Daure, the steward of provisions, because there was only bread for two days, whilst he had announced enough of it for four, when M. de Chastellux had to commence his march the next day. I do not like this steward, nor, in general, the superintendent of the provisions, who is too pretentious and often hinders business by his scrupulous formalities. But, at present, M. Daure was not at all in the wrong; without vehicles, without wood, in a country absolutely stripped of everything, where it was necessary to create everything, it was impossible for him to do better; and M. de Chastellux was not only unjust at that time, but he had not the manner of a philosopher or of a man of quality.

On the 28th, the French and American troops came in front of Yorktown, four leagues from Williamsburg, where Cornwallis had shut himself up with his whole army. They took post half a league from the city and invested it, which was done without opposition. I remained at Williamsburg, where our principal establishments were, and where it was often necessary to provide for the service of the hospitals : I had 300 sick persons and a single employee; of these 300 sick, 10 officers were harder to please than all the rest.

October, 1781. I learnt that some reconnaissances had already been made in front of York. M. Drouillet, an officer of the regiment of Agénois, was wounded there, and a hussar of Lauzun's legion was killed. The English also abandoned some redoubts without resistance. On the 3d, I was five miles from Williamsburg at Trubell Landing to witness the landing of our heavy artillery, and some other effects which we were impatiently expecting. To day a body of English troops which occupied Gloucester, opposite to York, desired to prevent M. de Lauzun and M. de Choisy, who commanded at this point, from occupying a position where they wished to encamp. M. de Lauzun charged them with the cavalry of the legion and drove them back; it was Tarleton, a partizan, very well known in America, who commanded the English; he was wounded and thrown from his horse and had 50 men killed or wounded. We lost 3 men and 11 were wounded, 3 of whom were officers, among whom was M. de Dillon.

I learnt these details on the 4th, on going to the camp; but I was obliged to return the same evening. It was already cold and I made a fire on the 5th. I learnt that the English admiral Digby, who was expected from Europe with a strong squadron, had arrived with only three vessels, two of which were in a bad condition. We also learnt that the English had a vessel so much damaged in the last engagement with M. de Grasse, that they had been compelled to abandon it and burn it at sea. M. de Grasse, nevertheless, spoke with much modesty of this engagement, and I heard him say that it was only an encounter between two advanced guards.

On the 6th, I went to the camp in the evening. The trenches were open on this same day. I trembled lest it should be murderous, for we had not the means to afford assistance! I spent the evening with some officers of the artillery and of the engineers, who were awaiting the result. At nine o'clock, a pretty brisk fire was commenced at the attack of the left. There we had an artillery officer dangerously wounded and also six grenadiers wounded. On the right there was a soldier wounded. I visited the ambulance and an especial depot which I had placed near the trenches, to which I had gone as near as possible. I saw the city perfectly well and the English flag which was floating upon the intrenchments.

On the 7th, I returned in the evening to Williamsburg and continued to attend to the hospital which was becoming filled. It is nothing to see the unfortunate when we can render them assistance ; but it is cruel to be unable to aid them, and this is what I experienced. The effects and the employees of the hospitals had not yet arrived, and they could not have arrived, owing to the forced marches which we had made, half by land and half by water. We might at least have been able to land the effects indispensable for the service. I had made the remark. But the generals rarely listen to the administrators, when they do not themselves possess the spirit of foresight.

I learnt on the 8th that we had had only 5 or 6 men wounded in the trenches.

On the 9th we commenced discharging our batteries at night ; on the 10th, in the morning, the fire became very brisk and was kept up all day; we had artillery of the first class, and the Americans, for their part, had large cannons and displayed great activity; but they did not approach the perfection of our gunners, who were the admiration of General Washington; it is true they had perfect instruments, so to speak; the cannons were new and the balls perfectly suited to their calibre.

In busying myself to-day about something connected with my employment, I had occasion to enter the trenches, in a place where a mortar-battery had been established, which was firing upon one of the redoubts of the enemy; it replied with some howitzers which did no damage. I mounted this trench with M. de St. Simon, who commanded it, and to whom I had occasion to write, some days before, a pretty decided letter; we exchanged some friendly explanations. Some deserters from the enemy came to us, who told us that our fire greatly annoyed the English. According to their account, it was suspected that Cornwallis desired to escape; it would have been possible for him to do so by passing, during the night, across to Gloucester, but where would he have gone? He had a long journey to make to reach Carolina, where the English held some places; he ran the risk of perishing from want.

Next day, the 12th, our batteries set fire to an English ship of 44 guns.

During the night of the 11th – 12th, they made
the second parallel, which caused the wounding of
only two or three men. I was at Williamsburg, always busy about our sick men ; I had four hundred
of them and thirteen officers. Besides there was always
the same want of assistance ; they required of me supplies for the ambulance, for M. de Choisy's division,
encamped in front of Gloucester; I found myself in
the most cruel embarrassment and on the eve of seeing
the service fail which was especially entrusted to me.
And that would have happened if we had not had at
this period from two to three hundred wounded ; that
might be. Therefore I could not think without distress of M. de Chastellux's remarks, of whom I had
required vehicles from the North river, only for carrying some effects, at the rate of 250 sick persons —
" We shall not have fifty sick ! " And already at the
beginning of the siege we had four hundred of them.
Fortunately I had procured some assistance, on my
own account, which allowed me to wait a little. At
last, on the 13th, some supplies reached me which I
made haste to send off for the army. I went thither
myself and lay in the tent of my friend La Chèze.
There was much firing during this night and twenty-
three wounded men were carried to the ambulance.
I again returned to the trenches, in a battery from

which we discovered very plainly all York river, Gloucester, the English buildings and three of our ships which formed the entrance to the river.

In the evening we carried, by main force, two redoubts, which were captured in an instant, one by the French, the other by the Americans. The former were commanded by the Baron de Vioménil, having under him the younger M. de Deux Ponts; the latter by M. de la Fayette, having under him M de Gimat, an American colonel, a Frenchman by birth. We lost during our attack about 30 men killed and 60 wounded, of whom three were officers of the regiment of Gatinois and M. de Lameth, assistant quarter master general and nephew of Marshal de Broglie. I spent two or three hours at the ambulance in the midst of these wounded, a part of whom I despatched to Williamsburg. At this time I had more than five hundred sick, of whom twenty were officers.

I received some details respecting the attack upon the two redoubts. Our soldiers displayed great courage and liveliness. The English had about two hundred men in the redoubt attacked by the French; they made one or two charges before abandoning it, leaving only thirty men in it, who surrendered at the instant when our party penetrated into the fort. The Americans met with less resistance than we and lost only six men.

On the 16th, I intended to go to the camp and to dine with General Washington, who had invited me, but many wounded men reached me, which compelled me to remain at Williamsburg. They had been in a sortie which the English had made on the night of the 15th–16th, and in which at first they had been successful. They spiked four cannons and took a captain of the regiment of Agenois prisoner, but our troops soon rallied and the English were repulsed. Our works were nevertheless continued vigorously; we fired upon the English by ricochet, which greatly annoyed them, and they might have feared being captured sword in hand. Therefore, on the 17th, at noon, they asked to capitulate and the firing ceased. M. de la Chèze had the kindness to send me word of it immediately; I greatly rejoiced at it as a citizen, and also for this especial reason, that I perceived in this capitulation the end of our uneasiness respecting the service of the hospitals. There were still some difficulties respecting the articles of the capitulation; they even recommenced firing. At last, on the next day, the 18th, at noon, everything was concluded. Cornwallis surrendered as prisoner of war with all his troops, amounting to a body of 8000 men. It was not until the next day, the 19th, that they defiled in front of our troops and the Americans. Cornwallis said that he was sick and did not appear. The general who commanded in his stead wished to give up his sword to M. de Rochambeau, but he made a sign to him that he ought to address himself to General Washington. The English displayed much arrogance and ill humour during this melancholy ceremony ; they particularly affected great contempt for the Americans. Being detained elsewhere by our service, I was unable to be present at this spectacle, which would have greatly interested me.

On the 21st, I went to see the city of York. I visited our works and those of the English ; I perceived the effect of our bombs and balls. I made this visit with M. de Vioménil, who had been to see Cornwallis, who had not yet appeared ; he had even sent a refusal to Mr. Washington, who had invited him to dinner. M. de Vioménil invited him, and the English general accepted. M. de Vioménil invited me to this dinner, but having accepted an invitation to M. de Chastellux's, I was obliged for this day to decline. I regretted that I could not be present at this first meeting of Cornwallis with the French and American generals. He behaved well there and praised our troops, especially the artillery, which he said was the first in Europe.

M. de Rochambeau had gone to-day on board of the *Ville de Paris* to see M. de Grasse for the purpose

of thanking him and conferring with him ; it is certain
that we were greatly indebted to him. But it was
time for the siege to end. M. de Grasse spoke of going
away.

M. de Lauzun was entrusted by M. de Rochambeau
with the carrying of the news of the capture of York
to France and he embarked on the same day on the
Surveillante. I saw him at the moment of his departure ; he perceived me, got off his horse and asked
me what were my commands for France.

The English and Hessian troops, prisoners of
war, also left the camp ; they were very fine-looking
men. There was also a battalion of English grenadiers
of great height and good appearance. The remainder
of the English were small ; there were some Scotch
troops, strong and good soldiers. They proceeded
towards Williamsburg. I went to visit their camp ;
I saw them make their soup, go for wood, etc. The
Germans preservéd order and a certain discipline ; on
the contrary, there was very little order among the
English, who were proud and arrogant. There was
no call for this ; they had not even made a handsome
defense, and, at this very moment, were beaten and dis-
armed by peasants who were almost naked, whom they
pretended to despise and who, nevertheless, were their
conquerors.

Nothing new occurred until the 27th. Our troops were still at York and its vicinity. Cornwallis dined with General Washington and, successively, with all the French generals. On the 24th, M. de Deux Ponts set out for France on board of a frigate; he was charged by M. de Rochambeau to transmit to the ministry the statement of the corn which he demanded for the army. He required of the intendant a memoir for M. de Villemanzey and me and added to the note which the intendant had given me " an accomplished person of the greatest distinction. "

The weather changed from cold to warm; but the temperature was much milder than that of Rhode Island. The climate of Virginia is much more temperate.

At this time the regiments which M. de Grasse had brought with him from our island reëmbarked.

There was some conversation between the French and American officers. These latter seemed displeased at the civility shown to the English prisoners, who, for their part, were very attentive to us. The quarrel also arose from the fact that the French were forbidden to purchase some goods that were in York, whilst liberty to do so had been allowed to the Americans; undoubtedly, the motive was that the latter, being in want of everything and badly paid, had been desirous of being allowed to buy merchandise cheaply.

November. The last of October and the first days of November were fine; the nights were cool, with white frost; but by day the sun shone and it was even fine. At the same period last year at Newport we had snow and very sharp cold.

The troops went into winter quarters on the first of November. Part remained at York; the remainder came to Newport[1] where M. de Rochambeau established his head quarters. I secured a very pretty lodging there, where I settled myself with my friend La Chèze. We kept a very good house there; and altogether we led a very pleasant and quiet life, but not very fruitful in events. Therefore my journal is about to become barren.

M. de Grasse had sailed on the 4th, and the frigate which conveyed M. de Deux Ponts, having been delayed for some time, went away on the 1st.

On the 22d a pavilion took fire, which was attached to the hospital for the officers, then amounting to twenty-two, of whom several were severely wounded. We had time to remove them elsewhere without any accident and lost only a few goods. This pavilion

---

[1] In Virginia.

was distant only 5 or 6 toises from the large hospital which, fortunately, was not reached.

December, 1781. Another fire broke out a short distance from the American hospital, which was burnt up in a short time. A sick soldier perished.

January, 1782. The weather grew warm from the early part of January and seemed to announce the spring.

On the 5th, we learnt the capture of St. Eustacia by the Marquis de Bouillé. The arrival of Monsieur de la Mothe-Piquet at our islands and ten ships also mentioned. This event and these new circumstances seems to promise us the peace which we began to desire.

On the 7th, the French frigate la Sibelle anchored at the entrance of the bay. Having left Brest in the end of October, she met near the Bermudas with a French vessel which had informed her that the French army was in Virginia. She was entrusted with two millions for us : she brought the news of the birth of a dauphin. On the same day letters reached us from Philadelphia, announcing the sending of a French corps of 4000 men to Minorca, to capture that island, jointly with the Spaniards. On the 10th we received our letters which came by the Sibelle.

The sudden changes of the weather in this province, as in the north, must be injurious to agriculture ; for instance, it does not seem to me possible in such a climate to have olive trees and vines, which the warmth of the summer would recommend to the cultivator. We had cold weather on the 5th and the 9th ; my ink and my wine froze in my chamber, where I had fire continually ; the next day we sometimes had 16° above zero.

February, 1782. At this period I finished a great many letters and transmitted them to the Baron de Vioménil, who was preparing to start for France with some officers on board of the frigate Hermione. She set sail on the 2d, at the same time with the frigate Diligente, commanded by M. de Clumard who proceeded to Boston and who ran aground owing to the fault of the pilot. M. de Clumard succeeded, with great difficulty, in saving himself and his crew ; twenty-three sailors or soldiers perished from cold and fatigue ; the vessel gradually disappeared and it was impossible to save anything from it.

March. The news of the capture of the island of Saint Christopher by M. de Grasse, which was spread for some time past, was confirmed. Two engagements between M. de Grasse and Admiral Hood, in which we had the advantage, were also mentioned.

The weather had the same successions of cold, snow, light rain and very fine weather.

M. de la Luzerne arrived at Williamsburg on the 25th ; I received him at dinner. He had just learnt from some English papers that a great convoy which had set out from Brest, escorted by M. de Guichen, had been scattered by a gale of wind and that the English had captured a part of them ; M. de Guichen had been compelled to return to Brest, which must have greatly delayed the projected attack upon Jamaica.

April. The first days of the month were fine. I made a voyage to York. We had some letters which gave us no interesting news, except from our families. My wife and children were well.

May. No occurrences. The heat began to increase. We received news of some engagements between M. de Grasse and Rodney on the 9th and 18th of April ; but the truth gradually came to light. M. de Roch-ambeau, relying upon a worthless newspaper of Grenada, at first had cannons fired in token of victory.[1]

June. But about the 20th of June we learnt that, on the contrary, we had met with a defeat and that the *Ville de Paris* had fallen into the hands of the

---

[1] I have before me the Broadside which gives the details of the supposed victory. It is dated at *Martinique, le* 17 *Avril*, 1782 and is headed in large capitals, DETAIL DU COMBAT NAVAL DE M. LE COMTE DE GRASSE AVEC L'ADMIRAL RODNEY.

English.[1] I had one of the severe heart-aches to which I am subject.

At this period we prepared to set out for the North river, after being in winter quarters for eight months. The heat kept up between 28° and 30° from the beginning of June.

On the 23d of June, the first division of the army began its march.

July. I only started on the 4th of July with the fourth division, consisting of the regiment of Saintonge and a detachment of artillery, the whole under the command of M. de Custine. Baltimore was the point of reunion for all the troops. Our corps stopped and encamped on the first day at a place called Drinking spring, only nine miles from Williamsburg. The country is like the environs of this last mentioned city, that is to say, it is dry and covered with wood. We met with nothing there but Indian corn, apple trees and some peach trees. I saw very little tobacco there, although this is the chief production of Virginia, and the part which we were traversing, situated between the James river and the York river, is renowned for

---

[1] I have elsewhere cited the account of this disastrous battle as given by Count de Grasse. It is in the Archives of the French Navy Department and inscribed *Memoires du Comte de Grasse*, Nos. 15, 186 and 6, 397.

this crop; as to wheat, I saw only one field of it in Virginia.

On the 15th, we lay at Bird's Tavern. The country seemed to me to be still worse. I was pretty well lodged. I was billeted at the house of some Americans, who received us by private contract. This is contrary to their laws and usages: but, generally, they submit, with pretty good grace, to this unpleasant duty. As yet I had no sick persons; I was ordered to receive not only those of my division, but also the sick of the troops which marched in advance and who were left for me.

On the 6th, we stopped at Ratelof House. The country is still barren and sandy. On the 7th, we encamped at New Kent; it is not a village but the center of some scattered houses, distant from each other, in a county. I lodged at the house of a colonel whom I found rather unfriendly, like all my hosts; the women also seemed to me very unsociable. All these people lead rather a dull life, not knowing how to employ or amuse themselves. The dwelling of this colonel, moreover, was handsome enough and built upon a hill, with an agreeable prospect which is rare in Virginia, where the country is flat. A branch of the York river runs below the house, in a valley where it would be possible to form meadows; but all that is not understood by the Virginians. This valley is also watered by the Pamunky, a small river which resembles that of France and likewise empties into York river.

I have mentioned that we lodged in the houses of the Americans; but we only asked them for shelter. Every one took with him his provisions, his utensils, a bed and sheets and we put our hosts to no expense. For my own part I had two wagons or covered vehicles, drawn by good horses, and was in want of nothing. At any rate this kind of life was not displeasing to me. After having been on the road all morning, I spent the evening alone and quiet, often in handsome houses, given up to my reflections and happy in my own way.

On the 8th, after a long and painful march, we reached Newcastle ; our division encamped and remained there. The Pamunky flows alongside of this village. The Count de Viomémil, who had stopped there with the third division, gave a ball. He was lodged in the house of a resident who had a handsome dwelling and who derived a great profit from a stallion which was valued at two thousand guineas.

On the 5th, we reached Hanovertown, only five miles from Newcastle. This city is situated in a plain agreeable enough and of a pleasant appearance, where some handsome dwellings were seen. The principal

21

crops still consist of Indian corn and I saw no other products there. I except a small quantity of ordinary hemp. There are in this county some rich proprietors, having a great number of negroes. In fact, the inhabitants of these southern provinces do not cultivate their estates themselves, like those of the north; they have negro slaves, like our colonists in our islands, and they themselves lead an idle life, giving themselves no concern about anything except their table. In general, they are not equal to the people of the north, as regards morals and honesty, and in some respects they are two different peoples.

On the 11th, we arrived at Hanover Court-House. I made the journey by night. In the morning, as it began to grow light, I was struck by the beauty of five or six trees, grouped together on the bank of the Pamunky. I dismounted to measure them and examine them more attentively. They were twenty feet in circumference and about eighty feet high, and also straight and of handsome proportions. These trees, the handsomest that I have seen in America, were tulip trees.

On the 12th, an encamping at Brunksbridge. It had rained in the night so that we were not very warm. The country here is less cultivated and less cleared than in other parts of Virginia. So the habitations are rarer and poorer there. I was lodged in a house situated in the midst of the woods and where there are some very handsome fir-trees. I had not yet seen any in America of this height; in the vicinity of Williamsburg the fir tree is common enough; but it is of moderate height. I saw also in this place some handsome oaks, some fruit trees and especially peach trees; the roads are fine and solid.

On the 13th, we are at Bowling Green, a dry and barren country, as usual. Near our encampment is a handsome house, with terraced gardens and some artificial meadows in the vicinity. I saw clover mowed by some negro slaves, as I have mentioned. The dwelling house which we see has not less than eighty; the species greatly multiplies there. The children, boys and girls, go naked until ten or twelve years old; the others have nothing but a shirt or some miserable rags.

On the 14th, we encamped twelve miles from Fredericksburg. I walked in the surrounding woods; this country seemed to me below mediocrity, wherefore it is thinly inhabited.

On the 15th, our division passed through the city of Fredericksburg without stopping there; it crossed the Rappahanock river to go and encamp on the other side, that is to say at Falmouth; this town is not much, but Fredericksburg is considerable. The Rappahanock is not very broad, very nearly as the Seine at Paris. We could ford it there : but for fear of accident all the vehicles were transported upon ferryboats, which are large and very convenient in America.

Mr. Washington's mother and sister reside at Fredericksburg. Our generals and several officers visited them. I left a hospital establishment at Falmouth ; we had sixty sick men there. To-day, the 15th, I dined at M. de Custine's. I mention it because he was lodged in a handsome house, situated upon a hill from which we perceived the course of the Rappahanock and the cities of Falmouth and Fredericksburg which made up a pretty brilliant prospect rather rare in America.

On the 17th, the division marched ; they encamped near a tavern called Peton's Tavern ; the road to it is hilly, in a barren country. I went to lodge three miles beyond the camp in a place where the country was more agreeable. The house where I was is situated in a valley where there was an orchard planted symmetrically ; the apple trees in it were covered with fruit.

On the 18th we came to *Dumfries,* a little town situated two leagues from the Potomac and which is watered by one of its branches. I was lodged in the house of a young Irishwoman, twenty-six years old and pretty handsome; she told me that her name was Margaret * * * and that she was of the family of this name, settled in France and that she had a brother, John * * * in the French regiment of Walsh. Her husband, * * * * * * was a Scotchman; she seemed far from being rich, although well lodged. I found her manners easy and European. She did not come to America until she was seventeen years old and she seemed to desire to leave it. In the evening I introduced to her one of her fellow countrymen, an Irish priest, the Abbé Lacy, the chaplain of our hospital, whom she received very well.

The weather was cooler; it seems to me that from this part we begin to feel a difference in the temperature which perhaps arises from the country's being mountainous and intersected by numerous rivers.

On the 19th we encamped at Colchester after having crossed the Occoquon, which is a branch of the Potomac. This town is small and miserable as well as the country. A horse had been stolen from me at Dumfries. I strongly suspected the people of my amiable Irishwoman, about whom I learnt nothing good, any more than about her husband, who is considered an adventurer. The woman is accused of some gallantries, which is rare in America; besides, she was born in Europe.

On the 20th we stopped at Alexandria, a city situated upon the Potomac, where ships of fifty guns can approach. This city is perfectly well situated for becoming commercial. Therefore they have built much there; it may become considerable, still it is not much. General Washington's residence, that in which he was born, is situated between Colchester and Alexandria. Mrs. Washington had arrived there the evening before. She invited M. de Custine, who commanded the division to which I was attached, to go and dine at her house with some officers. He proposed to me to go thither and we proceeded thither, to the number of ten persons. Mrs. Washington is a woman of about fifty years of age; she is small and fat, her appearance is respectable. She was dressed very plainly and her manners were simple in all respects; she had with her three other ladies, her relations. As to the house it is a country residence, the handsomest that I have yet seen in America, it is symmetrically built and has two stories, counting the false roofs, wherein some pretty chambers have been constructed. All the rooms are furnished with taste.

There are in the places around, many huts for the negroes, of whom the general owns a large number, who are necessary to him for his large possessions, which are supposed to amount to ten thousand acres of land. (The acre is very nearly of the same extent as our arpent.) Among these some of good quality is found, and I have observed some of it of this sort. A large part is woodland, where Mr. Washington, before the war, enjoyed the pleasure of the chase, which had inclined him to the military life which he has since led. The environs of his house are not fertile and the trees that we see there do not appear to be large. Even the garden is barren. What decided the general's parents to choose this dwelling place is the situation which is very handsome. The Potomac flows at the foot of the garden and the largest ships of war can anchor there. It has different branches of a kind of bays and in this place is about half a league broad. The whole make a very agreeable prospect. The opposite shore needs rather more houses and villages. Taken all together, it is a handsome residence and worthy of General Washington. In the evening, we left her respectable company after having spent a very agreeable and truly interesting day.

On the 21st, we crossed the Potomac; the camp was placed at Georgetown, a small town, wherein many German families are found. We then leave Virginia and enter Maryland.

On the 22d, an encampment at Bladensburg ; this town is small, but agreeably situated and surrounded by meadows; there are some handsome houses built upon the hill. I was very well lodged in the house of the judge of the place, named William Anderson ; he had a handsome family with whom I took tea. On the 23d, we received the bad news of the capture of one of our convoys bound to the Indies and of two ships which were escorting it. We were all distressed at it, we saw peace still remote.

On the 25th, encampment at Rose Tavern. A march through a country more cultivated than in Virginia, but still middling. I lodge at the house of a very rich resident named Major Smoden. His wife invited me to dine and seemed to me genteel, with the air of a good education, although she had never left her own country ; she had a daughter equally well bred. I taught them some words of French. The husband did not come until the evening; I also supped with them. A piece of ham was served up to us, as at dinner. They informed me that they eat it at breakfast, dinner and supper. Indeed bacon is very common in all this region and is very good food. Major Smoden's house is situated near a little river called the Patuxet, which we crossed yesterday at a ford.

On the 24th, encampment at Spurier's Tavern. All

this country is bad and the buildings indicate poverty. To-day, after dinner, I saw a humming bird very distinctly. I knew that they were in North America, and several persons had already seen them; but this was the first for me. I easily recognized it from the description that had been given to me; its small size, its quickness, its beak and its colors are remarkable; it makes a noise in flying and at first one might suppose that he saw that insect which is called *demoiselle* in some provinces of France. They are not larger; it has also a peculiar way in flying, that is to stop suddenly without moving its wings. I also saw it place itself upon a shrub and very near me; finally I had the pleasure of seeing it for a long time.

On the 27th, we arrived at Baltimore, where we stopped, as likewise all the army. This city is situated upon a creek which leads to the bay; it is commercial. After Boston and Philadelphia it is the most important city of America. From thirteen to fourteen hundred houses and from eight to nine thousand inhabitants are counted there. They are building much there and this city will become flourishing. We had caused all our sick men, as well from York as from Williamsburg, to be transported to it by sea; we also brought a certain number of them, so that I was

22

obliged to establish a pretty considerable hospital, a part of which was made of boards.

August, 1782. It is said that peace is seriously considered. The English then sent back a large number of American prisoners. In the meanwhile, M. de Vaudreuil, coming from St. Domingo, appeared in these seas with thirteen ships of the line and, after having cruised for some time, he brought to Boston five vessels laden with wheat and masts which he had taken from the English; but one of his ships of war ran aground on entering the harbor of Boston and was entirely lost. The frigate l'Emeraude, coming from Newport to York, captured an English brig. All our heavy artillery left at York was brought to Baltimore, where we found ourselves all reunited! But this was for a short time, Mr. Washington having insisted, notwithstanding the rumor of peace, that the army should make a movement. In consequence, M. de Luzern set out on the 23d of August and proceeded towards Philadelphia. The other divisions had orders to follow and to set out successively. I was attached to the last, which started on the 27th, which gave me a little time to recover from a tertian fever, of which I had a violent attack during our stay at Baltimore. I have, therefore, few notes respecting this city and what occurred while we remained there. These fevers, moreover, were very prevalent in our army at this time and I believe that Baltimore is unhealthy, especially in the low part which I occupied and which borders on the marshes. I ought not to forget to mention that our troops were admired by the inhabitants of Baltimore for their handsome bearing and their manœuvres, and, indeed, I was surprised myself that, after a march, so painful owing to the dust and the great heat, they found themselves in so good a condition. I have not seen a better review at the camp of Compeigne. We had been in America nearly two years and our soldiers had become stronger; we had not a recruit, for the men who had been sent to us from Europe were all disciplined and drawn from old regiments. At one manœuvre a gun happened to be loaded with a bullet and a woman had her thigh wounded. She was an Acadian, about thirty years of age; she was well attended to and her wound was not serious. I remark, on this occasion, that there is at Baltimore a quarter entirely composed of Acadian families, where they speak nothing but French.

On the 27th we started and encamped twelve miles from Baltimore at Great Falls; I made the journey in a cabriolet, being still very weak.

On the 28th, a station at Burchtown. The country since leaving Baltimore is very thickly wooded and little cleared ; we see upon the road many brooks and ponds which serve to keep some foundries going ; there are some districts of handsome wood ; in another, it has been cut down, but it does not spring up again.

On the 29th, our division reached the banks of the Susquehannah, a river which empties into the Chesapeake bay ; it is two miles broad at this place, so that all our vehicles could not cross it in the ferry boat on the same day and we were obliged to remain at this place. This river is usually crossed at a ford, two leagues above the place where we were; but this passage is not free from difficulty and danger. It has been proposed to build a city on the right bank and near the ferry where we crossed it. It should be called Havre de Grace.

On the 31st, station at the Head of Elk, a town situated upon a small river which empties into the bay exactly at its extremity. It is there that I embarked when we proceeded towards York. Elk is in a very dry soil ; one is drowned with dust there. Fever is very prevalent there, doubtless caused by the swamps in the vicinity.

September, 1782. On the 1st of September we encamped at Newport, a small town situated on a creek, which communicates with the Delaware and is navigable. Newport is in the state of Delaware ; we leave Maryland between this town and the Head of Elk. This district is pretty well cultivated; but the land there is equally poor and sandy.

On the 2d, encampment at Chester, a small borough situated on the Delaware, fifteen miles from Philadelphia and in Pennsylvania. Half way between Newport and Chester we meet with Wilmington which belongs to Delaware, and where the assemblies of this state are usually held. This city, built of brick, a mile from the Delaware, is as large as Williamsburg and capable of growth. A mile from this city we find the Brandywine, of which I have already spoken, famous for the battle which the English gained there over General Washington; for he has lost some battles, but, like Coligny, he seemed greater after defeats and has never been discouraged.

The Brandywine is also remarkable for its large water mills, which the grain of Pennsylvania supports. In this district, and especially below Chester, the Delaware makes swamps of the water left by the sea upon this shore, which is very low.

On the 3d we were at Philadelphia. M. de la Luzern, who was still there as ambassador of France, offered me a lodging at his house, which I accepted; I remained there until the 5th.

On the 6th we proceeded to Trenton where the army

was concentrated into two divisions, instead of four. I remained attached to the last. I was not entirely recovered from my Baltimore fevers; therefore after having run about and attended to my official duty, as soon as I arrived at the lodging which was intended for me, I rested and kept quiet. Thus, my journal was almost laid aside. I will only say that we were not far from New York. We marched in military manner as far as the banks of the North river, where we arrived on the 15th. I had some good lodging places, and especially in [New] Jersey, where there are many Dutch families. I lived alone there and was happy. In this province, I also heard an inhabitant mentioned, named Blanchard. It was then said that M. de Suffren had defeated the English in the Indian ocean.

On the 16th, I crcssed the North river and caused my sick men, amounting to more than a hundred, to be taken across. I placed them in the Peekskill temple, where I had already established hospitals in the previous year. In going to it, I passed near the camp of the Americans, who then formed a body of six thousand men; almost all of them were clothed and in uniforms; their camp was adorned with leaves, which presented an agreeable appearance.

Our troops also crossed the North river and the head

quarters were established at Peekskill. The American troops were made to manœuvre in our presence, and they seemed very well drilled; it was the work of five or six months; for, a year ago, these troops were utterly disorganized and without any sort of instruction. This proves that we probably attach too much importance to our manœuvres, especially certain colonels of excessive zeal. It is Baron Steuben, a German by birth and a general in the service of America, who had contributed the most to forming and exercising the American troops.[1]

On the 20th we learnt that the Gloire, a frigate coming from France, had happily arrived at Philadelphia. The Aigle, another frigate, which accompanied her, under the command of M. Desouches, being pursued by the English, had been desirous of going through a place where the Gloire had not met with any accident; but, apparently, drawing more water, she touched upon a sandbank and ran aground. They had time to send the money and the passengers ashore; but the English captured the frigate, the crew and

---

[1] The Biography of Steuben (*Leben Von Steuben*, Berlin, 1858), and also that of *de Kalb* have been written by the Hon. Frederic Kapp, member of the imperial German parliament, with rare pains and impartiality. Translations of both of these interesting books have been published at New York.

the captain. Considering the frigate too much damaged, they set fire to it. The passengers who arrived by this frigate were the Baron de Vioménil, the Duke de Lauzun, and the Marquis de Laval, who had left us after the siege of York, the Prince de Broglie, the Marquis de Segur and some other young people of the court, who came to America for the first time. Some days before, the two frigates had had a glorious engagement with a ship of seventy-four guns.

On the 22d, in the evening, we had our letters. As to political news, always an uncertainty respecting the peace; some projects as to Gibraltar, the departure of the Count d' Artois for this place and the war of Geneva.

On the 24th, our army proceeded to Crampond, about nine miles from Peekskill; that of General Washington, being encamped upon the banks of the North river, made no movement. I remained at Peekskill, not being attached to the moving hospital near the army, which was then near to Peekskill, to have the sick forwarded to it.

October, 1782. The army remained in this position about a month. Putting it in motion was several times under consideration, and I believe that General Washington desired it; he had the siege of New York always in view, but he needed additional forces.

Finally, it was decided that our troops should approach Boston. It began to be said that we were about to embark upon M. de Vaudreuil's squadron, and proceed to the West Indies or some other point. This idea caused a fermentation in men's minds and especially in mine; for I desired nothing so much as to go to Saint Domingo to see my uncle.

The first division left the camp of Crampond on the 22d, and the second, on the following day. They stopped at Salem, which is also in the province of New York. I write this on the 23d and the weather is so fine that I am working in my shirt sleeves; to night I shall be obliged to put on garment over garment.

I had divined it, for it is very cold to-day, the 24th. I was obliged to get off my horse and walk on foot to keep myself warm. At the end of some miles we found ourselves in the road which I had passed over eighteen months before We passed by Richbury and stopped at Danbury; it is a pretty large town where, three or four years ago, the English committed great disorders, which are still visible. There are some pretty valleys in the neighborhood, some hills and rocks which remind me of Pégou near Angers.

I believe that I ought to mention here a rather remarkable occurrence that happened to M. de Roch-

23

ambeau soon after his departure from Crampond. His host, named Delavan, who was said to be of French origin, demanded a considerable compensation from him for some damage that the army had done him by encamping upon his property; his demand was exorbitant, it needed examination; but this man was unwilling to wait, he complained to the judge of the county and to the sheriff; the latter in conformity with the laws made his appearance to arrest M. de Rochambeau and, for that purpose, touched him on the shoulder. All those who were present desired to take him away; but M. de Rochambeau replied that he would conform to the laws of the country and he departed after giving security. However the plaintiff's charges were examined and reduced to one-half by the people of the country, but faithfully paid.[1] This incident shows the power of the law among the Americans and the good temper of M. de Rochambeau. I lodged at Salem in the house of the constable who arrested M. de Rochambeau. I did not know it then; he received me very well and made me take tea with him. He was a little old man, pretty lively. He had a daughter, not handsome and very familiar; one thing which shows this familiarity, but the American

---

[1] Paid by Rochambeau, we must understand.

manners at the same time, is, that having met her in the kitchen, she told me that she had left her room where the chimney smoked; I proposed to her to come into that which had been given to me. She agreed to it and remained there for a long time; sometimes we conversed, at other moments she suffered me to write and attend to my business.

On the 25th, our division proceeded to Newtown, a small town which I have mentioned, situated upon a hill whence the view is pretty agreeable. On the 27th, we took up our march for Breakneck : I met again, after more than a year, with all the places that I had passed through.

On the 28th, at Baron's Tavern, in a tolerably fertile valley which extends as far as Hartford. It is one of the best parts of America; so we found more readily what we needed, for instance, straw.

On the 29th, my division stopped at Farmington, and I proceeded to Hartford. There I saw M. de Tarlé, who confirmed to me the report of our approaching embarkation upon M. de Vaudreuil's squadron, to proceed to our colonies without a precise knowledge of our destination. He told me that I would embark with the troops and that they would give me another commissary of war as assistant. M. de Rochambeau also spoke to me to the same purpose.

On the 30th and 31st, the weather was frightful and the rain continual. The army remained at Hartford. I lodged at East Hartford, which is, in some sort, a second city upon the left bank of the Connecticut river. This country is very populous and entirely cleared; the soil is also good, and yet I suspect that the cultivation of it could be increased.

The army resumed its march on the 4th, in two divisions; it stopped at Boston on the 5th, at Windham on the 6th and at Canterbury on the 8th. On the 9th, the army proceeded to Watertown, where I saw the inn, Dorancy Tavern, of which the Chevalier de Chastellux gives so handsome a description in his travels, printed and well embellished. Moreover, the two young ladies of whom he speaks were no longer there and they both had houses of their own.

The inhabitants of this province, generally speaking, are more affable and more lively than those of Virginia. Our troops, upon arriving in their camp,

[Here there is a blank in the original manuscript.]

On the 11th we were at Providence, where I had spent so much time in 1780 and 1781. The entire army was quartered there until M. de Vaudreuil's squadron, in which we were to embark, was ready.

The artillery went first and set out for Boston, where it arrived on the 18th. I had already gone over this road, which is a fine one; we pass thereon through different villages and frequently meet with houses on it; yet the land there is pretty middling; it is the cattle, whom they feed there partly with maize, and some iron-works that make up the principal abundance of the country.

The next day I dined at the house of the consul, M. de l'Etombe. In the evening I was presented there to M. de Vaudreuil, and I worked during a part of the day with his son, the Chevalier de Vaudreuil, who served him as major.

On the 21st, there was a dinner at which I was present, given by Mr. Brick,[1] a wealthy American to M. de Vaudreuil and to several navy officers.

On the 22d I went to see the Commandeur Coriolis d' Espinousse, a relation of my wife and the chief of the squadron; he was residing five or six miles from Boston until his departure for France whither his health obliged him to return.

The Count de Rochambeau had transferred the command of the army to the Baron de Vioménil and set out on the first of December for Philadelphia, where he was to embark to return to France. M. de Chas-

---

[1] I have not succeeded in ascertaining who was the gentleman thus characterized as a " Brick."

tellux also started. Our troops arrived at Boston successively on the 3d, 4th and 5th of December; and they encamped in the order that they arrived. The weather was very fine, so that Dr. Cooper, the pompous protestant clergyman whom I have mentioned before, said " Heaven smiles upon the troops of France."

We then learnt that the expedition against Gibraltar had been unsuccessful.

On the 12th, the members of the assembly of Boston [1] came to congratulate the Baron de Vioménil, who received them in the midst of a large number of officers, of whom I was one. The spokesman, Mr. Samuel Adams, a respectable old man, spoke very spiritedly. His discourse and M. de Vioménil's reply were inserted in the public papers. On the same day the assembly gave a great dinner to M. de Vioménil and the principal officers of the army. It was Mr. Hancock, at that time the governor of the state, who presided at it.

On the 13th, in company with M. de Vioménil, I again went to see the Commandeur Coriolis d' Espinousse. We were in a boat; but the wind became so violent and contrary that we returned upon some bad horses which they had the kindness to procure for

---

[1] Massachusetts must be meant.

us in the district. Before reaching Boston we had to cross an arm of the sea which was half a league wide. It was so agitated that we were covered with water, and it was so cold that the water froze upon us. We were in danger, the water entered the boat in which we were, which our affrighted horses shook still more. But, some days afterwards, we returned thither to dine. He was making preparations to return to France, on board of a frigate wherein, upon my recommendation, he granted a passage to two persons.

We thought of starting on about the 20th; but we were still at Boston on the 22d, in consequence of some delays. The 22d was a Sunday; I mention it because, having walked through the city, I saw no one there. The inhabitants were in the temples or retired in their own houses; they do not allow the least recreation and do not visit. Moreover, this is the same almost everywhere in America. At Providence some amiable women, of a lively disposition, at whose houses I called, were even unwilling to sing on Saturday evening. In the month of September last, a pretty singular occurrence befel me, on going from Philadelphia to the North river, which proves this great strictness. Some officers came to see me on a Sunday and I proposed to them to play a game of revereis; the mistress of the house where I was lodging entered the room angrily and wished to snatch the cards from us. I had difficulty in quieting her and was obliged to have her told by the chaplain of the hospital, an Irish priest who spoke English, that it was not contrary to the principles of our religion to play cards on Sunday.

Boston is reckoned to contain 25,000 inhabitants. Its size is about that of Angers. The houses are mostly of brick, the streets are pretty wide and well laid out, especially the main street. There are also some unsightly quarters which give Boston an appearance less modern than Philadelphia and the other cities of America.

I have already mentioned that several families of the name of Blanchard are found there. One, very rich, of French origin, went from Rochelle to America after the revocation of the Edict of Nantes. Many families belonging to Rochelle did the same ; for there is a village in New York entirely built by the Rochellois. It is called New Rochelle.[1] Our army was pretty near to it in 1781 and several of our officers went to it.

---

[1] June 5, 1751. Joseph Shippen (afterwards colonel and secretary to the Province of Penn.) writes to his father, that President Burr (of the College of New Jersey) advises him to go to New Rochelle to pass some months for the purpose of perfecting himself in French. *MS.* in the possession of Hon. J. C. G. Kennedy of Washington.

At this time mention was made of a man who had killed his wife and his children and afterwards himself. These crimes are rare in America and this was the only one that I heard of during all my stay.

On the 23d of December 1782 I went on board of the Triomphant, with M. de Vioménil, and on the 24th the whole squadron, carrying the army, set sail and left the harbor of Boston; the channel is narrow and has little depth; so that we were not without uneasiness. Our pilot himself did not appear to be quite composed and incessantly repeated " to rig." However, we fortunately got through; one only of the transport ships, the Warwick, was shattered upon the rocks on setting sail; happily, there were no troops on board. We were to cruise as high up as Portsmouth, a pretty good port beyond Boston, where two ships of war were which were to rejoin us and then to cruise alongside of Rhode Island in order to meet with the Fantasque, a vessel armed *en flute*, to the wind. The bad weather changed these designs; we could not, without danger, remain upon these coasts exposed to being cast away upon them or driven upon sand banks.

On the 27th, the frigate Iris left us, to proceed to France. On the same day we lost sight of our convoy and our frigate. Moreover, every vessel carried a

24

sealed package pointing out the general destination of the squadron.

We thus found ourselves reduced to ten ships of war.

	Guns	Commanders
The Triomphant,	80	Mis de Vaudreuil,
The Coronne,	80	Mitton,
The Neptune,	74	Daltains,
The Northumberland,	74	Medine,
The Brave,	74	Damblimon,
The Souverain,	74	Glandeves,
The Bourgogne,	74	Champmartin,
The Duc de Bourgogne,	80	Charette,
The Citoyen,	74	Dethis,
The Hercule,	74	Ch^r De Bros.

The vessels remaining at Portsmouth and which were to start were the *Auguste,* of 80 guns, commanded by the Chevalier de Vaudreuil's brother, and the *Pluton,* commanded by M. d' Albert de Riom; they had with them the *Amazone,* a frigate which M. de l' Aiguille, the brother of the major of the squadron, commanded, and the *Clairvoyante,* Paché, commander. The weather was so bad in the first days that it was impossible for me to write, the rather as I had not a room and slept with thirty officers in the main cabin. I ate also at M. de Vaudreuil's table where we had ten or twelve. The rolling was so great during the first days that we were obliged to eat upon the floor.

January, 1783. To-day, January the 8th, we are at present in 27°; the heat is very great. Our destination is still a mystery, I do not even know if we have a positive one. One circumstance would make me believe so. We were joined on the 5th by a vessel which left Boston five or six days after us and which brought a letter from the consul to M. de Vaudreuil. This informed him that, shortly after our departure, an aid-de-camp of M. de Rochambeau had arrived, bringing some letters which he had been afraid to trust to this little vessel, but which he had sent to Portsmouth to be brought to us by the ships of war which were there and which were to rejoin us. He also mentioned that a frigate commanded by M. de Capellis had just arrived from France in the Delaware, after a passage of forty-five days; she, doubtless, brought orders from the court, which, perhaps, would have modified our route.

January 19*th*. The difficulty of finding a place for writing, prevents my keeping my journal regularly. To-day I have the means and I profit by it. We are near Porto Rico, an island belonging to the Spaniards.

We cruise there to collect the merchantmen and transports from which we were separated. Many have already rejoined us. We have chased two English frigates without success. Our prizes at present consist of only two brigs. According to their account and that of a frigate, the Aigrette, commanded by Cabanis, and the cutter, the Malin, commanded by Beauvais, anchored at Saint John of Porto Rico, the English are cruising with sixteen ships of the line alongside of the cape of Saint Domingo, from which we were not far distant; we had only ten vessels, therefore the match was not equal. On the other hand, they told us that the question of peace is under consideration. However we prepared to leave our cruising ground, to reach I know not what point, which M. de Vaudreuil keeps a secret. It seems to be a place of meeting agreed upon with the Spanish fleet.

Although we are still in the latitude of 20°, we do not find the heat too powerful. The sun is intense, but refreshing winds almost always prevail. On crossing the tropic, we had the usual ceremony. It is the carnival of the sailors, to whom it brings in some money.

Here is the staff of the Triomphant which I have not yet given.

M. de Vaudreuil, chief of the squadron.

Montcabier, flag-officer.

The Chevalier de l'Aiguille, major.

The Chevalier de Grimaldi, adjutant.

The Chevalier de Viola, adjutant.

The Chevalier de la Panouse, of the marines, assistant adjutant.

Repentigny and Desson, lieutenants.

Delange, Panat and Belzin, ensigns.

Mandat, de Dussus, le Pont and Moucheron, officers of the marines.

Three auxiliary officers and three officers of the regiment of Médoc, keeping garrison in the ship, who, with the officers who were passengers, made 55 persons.

The soldiers and sailors were in proportion, so that there were more than eleven hundred persons on board of this ship. We also had on board the famous Paul Jones, who had asked permission to embark on board of us and who behaved with great propriety.

At last we learnt, in the last days of January, that it was at Porto Cabello, in New Spain, Province of Caraccas, that we were to put into port. In order to reach it we were compelled to cruise for a long time between Curaçoa and New Spain. This is only a distance of ten leagues and is not free from danger. Bottom is easily found there and these channels were unknown to us. Our Spanish pilot did not appear to

be acquainted with them. The island of Curaçoa belongs to the Dutch ; we went sufficiently near to it to
have a good view of it. It is seven leagues in length,
the city seemed pretty and announces that cleanliness
which distinguishes the Dutch. One evening we approached the coast so closely that a cannon was fired
from the land to inform us of the danger which we
were running.

February, 1783. On the 8th, several of our ships
were obliged to put into port at Curaçoa, and we also
found ourselves separated from the convoy which we
had brought from Porto Rico. We were joined by a
French lugger, the captain of which came on board of
us. He informed us that the Bourgogne, a ship of
74 guns, which was a part of our squadron and of
which we had lost sight on the night of the 3d and
4th of February, had struck upon a sand bank, two
leagues from the Spanish coast, without being able to
get off. This lugger had been dispatched from Porto
Rico to bring assistance to the shipwrecked vessel and
had indeed succeeded, with a frigate and a small
Spanish vessel in saving three hundred men who had
remained on board of this ship, entirely destitute of
succor and food, for the vessel was half swallowed up
and was gradually sinking in the sand bank. This
captain told us that all the officers had perished in

endeavoring to land by means of long boats and rafts. As among these officers there were twenty of the regiment of Bourbonnois, and as we also had several of the same regiment on board of the Triomphant, who had relations and friends on board of the shipwrecked vessel[1] (I myself had my brother-in-law in it!) as in short we were exposed to the same danger on this unknown coast, this news was a clap of thunder for us all. Yet there are some doubts still as to the loss of the crew and we impatiently waited to land in order to know the truth. At last, on the night of the 10th, we arrived at Porto Cabello, where we anchored.

Since morning, we had perceived the high mountains which overlook this port and which do not present an agreeable appearance. The next day we landed and paid a visit to the assistant commandant of the Province of Caraccas, to the commandant of the city and to the administrator, the delegate of the intendant, who resides at Caraccas, the capital of the province.

We dined on the 12th at the house of M. de Nava, the assistant commandant of the province. The dinner, well cooked and abundant, composed of French

---

[1] The Chevalier de Coriolis, whose account of the loss of the Duc de Bourgogne, and the sufferings of the survivors has been printed by M. La Chesnais in the *Revue Militaire Français*.

and Spanish ragouts, was served on rich silverware. The city consists of nothing but huts, without ornament, without hangings, without furniture and only one story high. The commandant's house had several, with large rooms, but all quite bare.

At length we learnt from an officer of the regiment of Bourbonnois, saved from the shipwreck of the Bourgogne, and who arrived to-day, that only four officers were lost, of whom my brother-in-law was not one. I had the pleasure of seeing him the next day ; he had saved himself upon a raft. There was much disorder in this affair and the captain and some of the officers will always be reproached for abandoning the vessel and leaving three hundred soldiers and sailors in it.

After the above mentioned day, the 12th, I took up my quarters on shore, as likewise the superior officers of the army ; the troops remained on board. My duties did not amount to much, the whole being on account of the navy. My service consisted in keeping the army-chest, and remitting money to the different persons attached to the staff of our army, either as employees or officers.

The heat here is excessive. Porto Cabello is only the port of entry of the commercial company of Caraccas, situated thirty leagues from here. This com-

pany deals especially in cocoa, and that of Caraccas is
considered the best. It is also an excellent harbor;
the largest ships anchor at the quay. The country
would be able to furnish the best products of our
island, if it were cultivated; but the Spaniards are as
lazy here as in their native country. I have visited
some residences in the vicinity. I have seen there
the most beautiful trees, palms, citrons, oranges, ba-
nanas and cocoa-nuts; I have eaten some delicious pine-
apples there Several of our officers went to Caraccas, a pretty considerable city where there is good
society, and some very rich people. A bishop resides
there who has a considerable revenue.

March, 1783. The heat is excessive; almost all the
persons who lodge on shore became sick, and I was so
myself; my domestics likewise. De la Chéze's servant
died of fever, accompanied by vomiting. At last, on
the 24th of March, the frigate Andromaque arrived at
Porto Cabello and brought us official information of
the certainty of peace. The news was received with
delight. From this I except some little ambitious
grandees who think of nothing but themselves and
their own advantage. This peace, advantageous to
France, was disastrous to England, and it seemed to
all that if the former knew how to avail herself of this

25

prosperity, she might recover the superiority in Europe to which England pretended.

At last we thought of leaving Porto Cabello, which was becoming more and more injurious to our health. On the 2d of April I went on board of the Triomphant, with all my effects, where we again met with the same officers; there was no one in addition to them except the Chevalier de Roquelaure, an ensign, from the Bourgogne. On the 2d, I went to dine on board of the Souverain, commanded by M. de Glandeves, whom I had known in Corsica, an officer respectable for his accomplishments and talents. On the 3d, the squadron sailed, except the Triomphant, the Auguste and the Néréide, which did not set sail until the 4th. Having learnt that M. de Vaudreuil granted the frigate Amazone to the Count de Segur, in order to proceed directly to Port-au-Prince or to Jacmel, in the island of Saint Domingo, where he had a house (the squadron was to put into port at Saint Domingo, but at the cape). I obtained permission to go on board of the Amazone with M. de Segur. We had a very good wind and made a hundred leagues in three days. All this time was pleasant for us. M. de Gaston, the captain, treated us very well; he had with him two or three amiable officers and M. de Segur, really a man of wit, a poet and an interesting story teller, who added much animation to the conversation. We also had M. Berthier, an officer of the staff of the army, who accompanied M. de Segur. The officers of the navy were, with M. de Gaston, Du petit Thouars, his mate ; he is from Saumur ; he is an odd young man, but intellectual, zealous and devoted to his calling ; La Mothe Guillonnais, an ensign, and Boulen, an officer of marines, besides two auxiliary officers. There were also three officers of the regiment of the Cape, with a detachment from this corps which was in garrison there.

On the 8th, in the morning, we discovered the coast of St. Domingo ; it was the point of Salines in the Spanish part, forty leagues from the place where we were to land ; this point semed to be uncultivated and uninhabited. We were almost becalmed on this day, and we made very little headway the next day.

On the 9th, we perceived at the distance of three leagues a fleet of thirty sails, several of which were ships of war. We concluded that they were English on their way to the Windward islands and Jamaica ; that was the route. Hostilities had not ceased in these seas until after the 3d.

On the 11th, we had advanced very little, having no wind except at intervals ; we were, however, pretty

near the coast ; it is mountainous and we did not perceive many inhabitants.

On the 12th, having sent a boat ashore to a little
town which was in sight, we learnt that we were at
Jacmel. M. de Segur, M. Berthier and myself proceeded to it in a boat at four o'clock in the afternoon.
It is a small town of about fifty houses, where there is,
nevertheless, a military commandant, at whose house
we were put on shore. M. de Segur, being desirous of
setting out that evening, the commandant procured
some saddle-horses for us, and we started, after supper,
at eight o'clock for Leogane, which is fourteen leagues
distant. The road is mountainous, bordered by preci-
pices, cut up by torrents and very picturesque. It
was beautiful, clear moonlight, so that we enjoyed the
spectacle ; a negro served as our guide ; he went on
foot ; as he was tired and I had the best horse, he
mounted behind me. A league before arriving at
Leogane, we found a vast plain where there were several dwelling houses. We observed that of M. Michel,
called the Barbot residence. It was five o'clock in
the morning and daylight when we arrived at Leogane. This town is small, but pretty, with a handsome square. We dined at the house of M. de
Théridan, who procured carriages for us to proceed to
Port-au-Prince, distant seven leagues. We performed

this journey in three hours and a half and arrived at Port-au-Prince at nine o'clock at night. We stopped at the door of a large inn and I had not yet got out of the coach when an inhabitant approached. I recognized my uncle whom I embraced with transports of joy. He took me to the house of one of his friends, M. Prieur, whose house was in the neighborhood and where they were at supper when the noise of the carriage attracted his attention. In the evening he took me to his residence, situated a league from Port-au-Prince.

On the next day, the 14th, the Count de Segur, for whom my uncle had sent to the city, arrived and shortly afterwards departed for his residence, which was in the neighborhood. On the 16th, my uncle gave a great dinner of thirty covers in honor of him, which was admirably served by some negroes and negresses, making a very good appearance, the women in white with a kind of hoop-petticoats. This dinner was returned to us on the 19th and we visited M. de Segur's residence.

I pass over the recollections, altogether personal, of my stay at St. Domingo. They interest only my children to whom I have often related them.

The Cape is a city with broad and straight streets, but the houses of which have only a ground-floor.

They are of wood and the windows are without glass. Their appearance is not very agreeable. Even the greater part of the single storeys are not ceiled, in order to give more air, so that we see the woodwork and the roof which is of small boards. A few houses are covered with slates. There is, besides, much building and the city grows every day. It is deficient from the want of quays, which are entirely wanting. The church is neat and large.

On going to see one of my uncle's neighbors, we found him engaged in flogging one of the negroes, who had been detected in a fault. However, all the inhabitants do not treat them harshly, and some are even very good to them. But if more correct ideas are entertained in the colonies respecting the condition of the slaves, who are often treated with humanity, this condition is none the less cruel. I know that there is no registry kept of their birth and that they are not taken to church to be baptized ; the most part have no religious principles which no one takes the trouble to give them.

At last, I had to leave, and I proceeded to the Cape where the squadron was assembled. There I found the Baron de Vioménil, with whom I was to be employed. I also saw again my brother-in-law, Baptiste de Coriolis. I had hardly time to see the Cape, which is a considerable city, with stone houses, of two storeys. Much was said at this time of the visit which had been paid to this city, a few days before, by Prince William,[1] the son of the king of England.

On the 30th of April, I embarked upon the Northumberland, with M. de Vaudreuil and the Baron de Vioménil. Our squadron consisted of eight vessels only. The Couronne, the Triomphant and the Souverain received orders to proceed to Toulon and were not to start until some days after us. M. de Médine commanded the Northumberland and the other officers were :

Le Veneur, lieutenant.

Gombaut, Vasselot and Chauvigny, ensigns.

Bossard, lieutenant of a frigate and auxiliary officer.

Mouton, pilot with the brevet of lieutenant of a frigate.

Belfonds, St. Pair and de Baunay, officers of marines. We had very nearly the same officers as on the Triomphant, with the addition of M. de Segur.

On the 2d of May, we were still only ten leagues from the Cape. Calms prevailed which delayed us. On the morning of the 4th we were in the latitude of Cap-Aux-Sables, one of the Turks' islands; we had

---

[1] Afterwards William IV.

doubled them all before noon. This part of St. Domingo is encompassed by a multitude of islands. We were uncomfortable enough on board. I rented the cabin of our boatswain, situated on the poop in a good air, and I thus had a corner to write in, to retire to and to be alone, which is very agreeable. Thus I never was so comfortable on board, my room was my happiness. I was at liberty to go to bed when I wished to; it is usually early. I also rose at daybreak, then I went to walk upon the deck, where there were not many persons, and to breathe the fresh air. I then breakfasted with Caraccas cocoa. I dressed myself and remained in my room until ten or eleven o'clock; I then went down into the council-cabin, where the time was spent in conversing until dinner time. I ate, with eight or ten persons, at M. de Vaudreuil's table; we lived well. After dinner, I made up my party, I returned to my room, I conversed.

On the 9th, towards night, in ordinary weather, we saw, at about half a league from us, a water-spout, or otherwise a column of water which rose from the sea in a cloud or which fell into it out of a cloud. We distinctly saw the column of water, the motion of the sea and of the water to the point of connection between the column and the sea; this column appeared to rise.

On the 14th of May, we were in sight of the Bermudas. They are a string of several islands which may be about ten leagues in length; they belong to the English. The climate there is mild, and these islands are reputed to be healthy. The English send their sick thither to recover their health; there is, however, no harbor for ships of war; but they are an asylum for merchantmen and a place of resort for pirates.

After this period, nothing remarkable occurred. On the 16th of June, we perceived that the color of the water was changing, which showed that we were approaching land, although, according to our reckoning, we ought to be a hundred leagues from Brest. Between two and three o'clock we found bottom at eighty-five fathoms. It was supposed that we were forty leagues from Ouessant.

On the 17th, at eight o'clock, a sailor, who was in the tops, cried out " Land !" but it was the allurement of some louis which M. de Vioménil had promised to whomsoever should announce it first that made him see it; for we again proceeded for more than three hours without discovering anything. At last, shortly after noon, M. de Médine himself, the captain of the ship, saw a breaker, which was perceived and signaled at the same time by some other vessels. We imme-

26

diately ran up. This breaker is known by the name of The Saints ; it is situated at the entrance of the harbor, and is a very dangerous rock. We were a a league from it and it was time to tack about. An hour afterwards we saw the land quite distinctly. At last, at three o'clock we were in the harbor of Brest. Boats were immediately launched in the sea and we repaired to land. It was a great satisfaction ; but the matters of business to which I was obliged to attend, on my arrival, and which were already occupying me, prevented my feeling this joy so vividly.

We found fires in almost all the houses and warmed ourselves with pleasure. I was obliged to remain at Brest until the 2d of July, 1783. I bought a carriage and horses and set out by short stages. I did not arrive at Rennes until the evening of the 6th ; I spent a day there and was at Angers on the 9th at noon. My brother, whom I had notified, was awaiting me ; I passed through the city without stopping and proceeded immediately to Echarbot. I found my wife and children on the road. I do not speak of the pleasure which I felt on seeing my family again, after an absence of more than three years. These emotions, these feelings cannot be described.

INDEX.